T0329065

ZIMBABWE: THE BLAME GAME
Recollected Essays and Non Fictions

Tendai Rinos Mwanaka

Mwanaka Media and Publishing Pvt Ltd,
Chitungwiza Zimbabwe
*

Creativity, Wisdom and Beauty

Publisher: *Mmap*
Mwanaka Media and Publishing Pvt Ltd
24 Svosve Road, Zengeza 1
Chitungwiza Zimbabwe
mwanaka@yahoo.com
mwanaka13@gmail.com
https://www.mmapublishing.org
www.africanbookscollective.com/publishers/mwanaka-media-and-publishing
https://facebook.com/MwanakaMediaAndPublishing/

Distributed in and outside N. America by African Books Collective
orders@africanbookscollective.com
www.africanbookscollective.com

ISBN: 978-1-77924-317-1
EAN: 9781779243171

© Tendai Rinos Mwanaka 2023

All rights reserved.
No part of this book may be reproduced or transmitted in any form or by any means, mechanical or electronic, including photocopying and recording, or be stored in any information storage or retrieval system, without written permission from the publisher

DISCLAIMER
All views expressed in this publication are those of the author and do not necessarily reflect the views of *Mmap*.

Table of Contents

Contents

The Prologue

Zimbabwe: The Blame Game is a collection of what I might term interlinked creative non-fiction pieces and essays on Zimbabwe. It straddles different types of non-fiction writing like the journalistic, academic, and general non-fiction types, but always with a creative bend. Why a creative non-fiction book? I feel I wanted to interest the general readers more than, say, the academic establishment. With this is mind, I thought to follow the rigours of academic or journalistic type of writing might put off the general readers that I was targeting, and that's why I thought of writing the story of Zimbabwe in this simple, creatively focused, easy to read, sometimes laid back way. General readers might not want to deal with technical, fact-embossed, and stuffy matter you would find in academic or even journalistic writing. Such that, most of the writings in this book, explore the story telling genre to describe or explain what I am trying to achieve in these writings; and I am using these stories to create depth that I should have created with technical or factual analysis of the issues.

Zimbabwe: The Blame Game, in the beginning, came out as an off-shot to my earlier manuscript, *Notes From A Modern Chimurenga*. When I was writing *Notes From A Modern Chimurenga*, I also wrote some non-fiction pieces, that I thought didn't fit into this manuscript. *Notes From A Modern Chimurenga* is a manuscript of short stories, so I had to take out the non-fiction pieces from this collection and added a whole lot new material to create Zimbabwe: The Blame Game. As the title Zimbabwe: The Blame Game suggests, it centres on finding who to blame for Zimbabwe's problems and the processes of

1

undoing Mugabe. It specifically deals with the whys, and whos of Zimbabwe's problems. I know some people might feel to blame someone for Zimbabwe's problems won't get us anywhere anymore. This should be the beginning. We should realise how each of us has been to blame, have caused these problems, and in that way, we could have a good headway in trying to find the solutions. Our problem, as a nation, is we have acculturated in our psyche this idea that we can simply walk through any dark period, without having to talk about it. We did that with the liberation war. We just lied to each other that everything that happened then was forgiven. We faked a reconciliation that didn't hold much further after independence.

And in doing that we have always created some power-sharing entities that never really work because we don't simply trust each other, to begin with. We have had four power-sharing governments in the last 34 years, and none of which have solved the things that caused the enactment of those power-sharing entities. What does that tell us about our psyche? Are we incapable, as a country, as a people, as a party, to stand on one foot? Another easily seen phenomenon, of these power-sharing governments, (three of which) is that, it has involved the same individual or party. The question should be why the same person or party? In 1978, Bishop Abel Muzorewa and Ian Smith entered into the first power-sharing government, for their own ulterior motives. In 1980, ZAPU and ZANU entered their own power-sharing arrangement. It didn't last as they accused each other of something that, up to now, nobody has ever explored or talked about: an arms catch found on a farm that belonged to ZAPU. In 1987, Joshua Nkomo and Robert Mugabe entered into another unity government, mostly to stop the war in the Matabeleland regions. But the question is; did it solve some of the problems the Matabeleland people have always complained of? In 2009, we entered into another power-sharing arrangement between the MDC and ZANUPF, which both parties have always been complaining that it isn't working. The prime cause why all these unity governments have never worked is because we just enter into these arrangements without first talking or even afterwards. We simply don't talk to each other. Maybe; about the wrongs we did to each other and genuinely embrace each other and forgive each other. The only talks we do is in making these power-sharing entities, i.e. on who is going to take this and that ministry, and nothing else.

There are those who always say there are some things that we shouldn't talk about, that some things have to be caged inside, that some things, they feel by talking about them, would result in more disagreements and conflicts. If these things are that important, there are exactly the things that we should be talking about. If we can't talk about them, we will never know where we went wrong, and most likely, we are going to repeat the same mistakes in the future. Talking is the beginning of the search of solutions and the implementation of the solutions, and through talking we get to understand each other, and let the hurt, sorrow and pain be dealt with, and try to genuinely forgive each other and move forward. But we haven't been doing all that, and so, years later, these enforced reconciliations won't hold. This is what I am trying to encourage in this book, that we start the process of talking. We need to face each other with an open mind, honest engagement, with real love that doesn't just run along the path to judging, with forgiveness, with real reconciliation. For us to do that we need to start to talk to each other, but this collection goes further than Zimbabwe, than encouraging talking.

The Blame Game could be applied into other perspectives, other countries. It still tackles Zimbabwe, even as it tackles life in exile, especially for those Zimbabweans who left for South Africa; what they had to deal with, especially the xenophobia of year 2008. There are also two particular pieces that deals with South Africa, what I think is happening in South Africa, where I think South Africa is heading towards. It is the Zimbabwenisation of issues in South Africa that I am trying to explore, above everything else. The biggest import of those pieces on South Africa was to not only indict, but to give advice, so that; maybe, South Africa might regurgitate safely through its problems. The last few pieces in this book deal with Zimbabwe after the GNU negotiations and a look at the future for Zimbabweans and Zimbabwe. It also throws a light on Mugabe.

The piece that holds the book together and which the book borrows its title from is The Blame Game, which delves deeply into who is to blame for Zimbabwe's (and Africa in general) problems and demise. Though I had to draw from a number of experts and from Newspaper articles on the analysis and indictment, of the problems and the solutions, I also had to put across a lot of my own thoughts and opinions, understanding and observation of these issues.

What am I attempting to achieve in this manuscript? Assigning blame is the first thing I am attempting to do, but undoing Mugabe is the biggest thrust of this book. Nobody in his rights senses would disagree with the fact that Mugabe was the problem, is still the problem, would be the problem in the future, and that undoing Mugabe from our country's body politic and lives should be everyone's mission. Only by undoing Mugabe will Zimbabwe be free and renormalize again. Here it's not about whether I like or don't like him, whether he represents interests of this or that group of people. It's because he is the most divisive person in the country, or even in the whole of Africa. He is now more of a liability than an asset to the

4

country, even to those who support him. It is only for this reason that I think it should be everyone's task to make sure that he goes…, but he should go in a way that won't take the country to the brink again.

Zimbabwe's Political Mine-Fields

There are three regions that I would like to think constitute the political minefields of modern day Zimbabwe. In this piece, I am not trying to say all the other regions I don't mention here were not important in shaping modern day Zimbabwe but I am looking at the most decisive regions, and their entire effects on shaping modern day Zimbabwe.

Matabeleland has been the scene of the first concerted protest against Mugabe's autocratic rule. After the elections in 1980, the two major parties which won the biggest chunk of the votes, ZANU and ZAPU, agreed to enter into a "loose" unity government. A couple of years later, Nkomo it was said, had to wear a women's dress as he debunked out of the country to dupe the security establishment that was on his heels, after getting fired by Mugabe. Mugabe was accusing Nkomo and his party of hoarding a catch of military weapons found on a farm that belonged to ZAPU. After the furore surrounding the arms catch found on this farm that belonged to ZAPU, in the Matabeleland regions, most of the ZAPU leaders, just after less than two years in this government, resigned. They also felt they had been given powerless ministries in this unity government, and also that the government was side-lining its regions. Who planted that arms catch is a question nobody has tried to answer. But I should think Nkomo must have created a comical figure, a big mamma's figure in that dress. I can't help asking was it a mini-dress, or skirt? He left for the UK where he stayed in exile. ZAPU left the unity government and became the political face of the struggle, of the Matabeleland regions' protest and or war against Mugabe; or as others wants to put it, against the Shona ethnic group.

Matabeleland regions witnessed the cleansing of over 20 000 of its people by the government, and displacements of millions of people. These people were killed by the secret security operatives and the disbanded Korean trained Fifth Brigade Army, commanded by Perence Shiri. Who later became the Air force boss and one of the "touted" military junta leaders? Villages were cleansed in a matter of a day, and some people were buried alive in mass graves in the Matabeleland region. In the book, *Breaking the Silence*, compiled by the Catholic Commission for Justice and Peace and the Zimbabwe Legal Resources Foundation, there are a lot of recordings, of innocent people who were killed in cold blood, being accused of aiding the rebels. In one of the pieces in this book, a fully pregnant woman is beaten until unconsciousness and losses the baby that comes out as pieces, and her husband is killed. There were accused of aiding the rebels, which they said they were not doing.

For the security operatives and the army to accuse these people of this, it meant someone must have thought that the Matabeleland people were backing these rebels, and why is the question?

Matabeleland's leaders and the rebels were waging a recalcitrant war against Mugabe's alienation politics against the Ndebele people. I know it's a contentious statement for they are those who believe, or who now believe, that the fight had been about the Shona versus the Ndebele tribal groups. The two regions (Matabeleland and Mashonaland) and these two ethnic groups (Ndebele and Shona) have always fought, going back to generations. Growing up, I remember hearing stories, passed down through the generations from

7

our forefathers, of these fights; the pillaging of the Shona regions by the Ndebele people, way before the white settlers came; taking with them Shona women, food, domestic animals and all sorts of wealth. That, there was always tribal tension between these two tribal places, I have no doubt about that, but I would like to think it had mellowed over the years as the ethnic groups assimilated. To give weight to this argument, we have to look at both sides of a coin. If we say it was because of this tribal bile between these two peoples, it means it's either the Ndebele people naturally are tribalistic, or that the Shona people are suppressive of other tribal groups. I don't agree with these observation.

In my adult life I have made a lot of friends from this region, and I have never felt they were tribalistic, neither do I think the Shona people are suppressive. There were a lot of Shona people, by the time we got to be independent, who were permanent inhabitants of the Matabeleland regions, who had been staying there peacefully, for lifetimes. So also a lot of Ndebele people who were staying in the Shona regions without any huge tensions, but with some minor skirmishes. I know of a lot of women, a lot of Ndebele women who are married to Shona men in my rural village, in Nyanga, whom we stayed with peacefully. Even in both parties, in ZANU and ZAPU, there were people from the other ethnic group in these parties. I want to narrow it further.

There is the school of scholars and politicians who believe this tribal tension was created by the western governments (the UK and USA) against I don't know, Mugabe or the Shona people, maybe. Mugabe was more aligned to the communists in Russia and China, and they go further and say that the apartheid regime in South Africa fuelled this war by supplying the Matabeleland rebels with artillery, so also to other rebels in the Southern African countries, i.e., Angola's UNITA group and Mozambique's RENAMO. I am not going to argue against this school of thought. The point still comes back to; for these countries to get involved for or against in this issue, they both had ulterior motives, but they had to have something to work with, in the first place, which is the alienation politics of the government against the Ndebele people. I don't see any way they were going to succeed without this. If Mugabe and the government in Zimbabwe had been treating people and leaders of this region fairly, if the predominantly Shona ruling hierarchy felt the Matabeleland people deserved a pie of the country's wealth and governance, this wasn't going to happen. It also brings into light the fact that even the MDC nowadays, is labeled a western world's invention (the UK and USA). The fact that it represents the genuine interests of some Zimbabweans, even at that, the majority Zimbabweans by the last recognized election, doesn't matter.

All over the whole world, succession of regions from countries have been about this, alienation of an ethnic race or tribe by the other ethnic race or tribe (usually the biggest group) in a country's politics.

Why I still say it was alienation politics? I don't even think it ended with the unity government of 1987. There is still alienation of the Matabeleland people, even today. The only problem is that they don't have leaders who really represent them, or else there will be real tensions now. I will start of by asking why, after 25 years of unity government, between the Ndebele and Shona leaders in the government, or to narrow it further, between those two parties that constitute ZANUPF; why is it the Ndebele people would always be forced to content with the second vice-president position in the ZANUPF party, and the country. I can understand that law within a

9

context of about 10-15 years after the 1987 unity deals, but beyond that, it becomes questionable. Laws can be changed over time, why hasn't this law been changed? It means that as long as the law is not changed, as long ZANUPF is still ruling the country, nobody from the Matabeleland would ever be the president of the country. It's the first vice-president who would become the president of the country, in a crisis or through the party's leadership lines, and that post belongs to Mashonaland, or former ZANU cadres. It doesn't matter how good a Matabeleland leader is, the best he could aim for is the second vice-president slot. Is that not alienation, to start with.

I know the politicos would tell you that it doesn't matter now where a leader comes from because we were made into one people by the 1987 unity government, and if so, why not change the alienating law? I will delve further and say that even the Matabeleland region is the most underdeveloped of all the provinces in Zimbabwe. For an example; I have been hearing about the Zambezi Water Project from time immemorial, and nothing has materialised. Nothing has materialised even as Bulawayo has always suffered from acute water shortages. The talks about this issue only happens when an election is looming, so that promises are flighted left and right, and then after the election nothing happens, or the talks just waft into thin air, to resurface again in the next election period.

Industries are closing shops in Bulawayo and the Matabeleland region. The government is doing nothing much. There is no encouragement, by the government, to industries to set up shop in the Matabeleland. The white government had set up Bulawayo as the industrial capital city and Harare as the administrative capital, to create balance. But now, Harare has gobbled everything. Bulawayo is now a ghost industrial city as most industries relocated to Harare.

10

Even for those industries that are still functioning; most of the people who run these companies, or work in these companies, are from the Shona regions. The Matabeleland people even complain that their wealth, I mean wealth generated in these regions, is taken by the central government in Harare, and used to develop the Shona regions. That's why they even entertain the idea of creating a federal system of governance (new ZAPU's ideology) or breakaway (Mthakwazi ideology). For years, people from Matabeleland complained about this without any action from the government, and it has made the Matabeleland children feel there are not wanted by Zimbabwe's industry or the workplaces. Now, most of them don't stay beyond form 4 or 6. Beyond that, they would have left for South Africa or other countries, to work in menial jobs and industries. They know they always come second in their country.

After Matabeleland had fought this recalcitrant war for nearly 5 years, this war ended with Mugabe and Nkomo entering into a unity government. Thus, deciding again the destiny of Zimbabwe, for years to follow. Even though Nkomo went into this government with Mugabe to serve his people from Mugabe's killings, the Matabeleland people never accepted these agreements and waited for another time; which came with the birth of the MDC party. Matabeleland region is the only rural provinces to vote resoundingly for the MDC in the 2000, 2002, 2005 elections, though they let the guard down in the last election in 2008, where it is now shared by all the three parties. It could be because they have realised that their grievances would not be represented well by the MDC, who are now predominantly Shona-led. After some of the Ndebele people in the old MDC left, some might have felt there was no longer any good representation in this MDC, and that's why the other MDC (Welshman Ncube lead or

Arthur Mutambara lead) got a number of seats in this region, and nothing anywhere else in the country.

Matabeleland had also been on the forefront of the liberation struggle where Nkomo and the ZAPU-ZIPRA party and army waged war against Ian Smith's Rhodesian forces from Botswana, mostly into the Matabeleland regions. They also won the entire region in the elections that ushered black rule. Now, every political party in Zimbabwe knows that if it garners this vote, it is almost near half-way to winning the entire election. This area spans the provinces of Matabeleland South, Bulawayo, Matabeleland North, and the part of lower Midlands's province which is inhabited by the Ndebele people.

Manicaland is where the fiercest and strongest war of the liberation struggle was fought. You can still feel, in this eastern province of Zimbabwe, the sadness that lingers in its streams, lands, forests and vast mountains, which are still haunted by spirits and ghosts of the liberation struggle. It is this land that can claim that it created the liberation war, and give birth to it, than any other province. Most of the liberation cadres were from this province. When I talk of Manicaland, I am talking of the land that spans the districts of Nyanga, Mutare, Buhera, Rusape, Chimanimani, Chipinge and the Headlands. I can tell you personal stories of the liberation struggle through the eyes of a small boy, the bullets at night like red arrows, nights spent outside, sleeping under the sky, under the unblinking stars. The runs every day away from Smith's soldiers, eating food whilst running, and the political bases which were at our homesteads. The small jobs as Vanamujibha (little secret eyes for the liberation forces),the kicks we got from Smith's soldiers for lying to them that we had never seen Magandanga (the liberation soldiers), all of our little lives. Even Mugabe admitted that this province had suffered a lot than any other province during the war, and ironically, it was the same province that was giving him trouble in post-independence Zimbabwe. Mugabe raged against this province in one of his campaign rallies for the March 2008 elections, at Sakubva stadium, that Manicaland had given him rivalries for his position as the president of Zimbabwe over the past elections, and in that election campaign. It was for this that he was not happy with this province.

This province gave Zimbabwe; Bishop Abel Muzorewa, from Rusape area of this province who was a co-leader with Ian Smith in the last 1970's government which wanted to pre-empty the blacks' eminent rule; and in so doing, they incurred worldwide opprobrium and condemnation. Manicaland also gave, to the country, the first ZANU leader in the name of Ndabaningi Sithole, who came from the Chipinge area of this province and whom, it is alleged, Mugabe's camp later removed from the leadership position of ZANU (a precursor to ZANUPF) during the war; by putting on another Manicaland leader, Herbert Chitepo. But Sithole continued being a thorn in the flesh of Mugabe, over the years, by always winning the Chipinge constituencies from the ZANUPF, and his ZANU Ndonga party held these constituencies for most of post-independence Zimbabwe. There is this Chipinge saying that they will always vote "Pandongapo", meaning they will always vote for ZANU Ndonga come what may. Chitepo was later assassinated in 1975 in Zambia. Speculation has always been rife that it was due to rivalry for positions that he was assassinated, though the official position is that he was assassinated by the Rhodesians, who also arrested most of the political leadership of ZANU party. Nobody knows the real truth here. The Army General, Josiah Tongogara, was also assassinated in Zambia in 1979, and no one knows who did it, other than the usual scapegoat, the apartheid Rhodesians in the government in Zimbabwe. Even the hosting president, Kenneth Kaunda of Zambia, doesn't know who killed those two. But he also admitted that there was fierce fighting between the liberation forces, at that time, in Zambia (Kaunda was talking in a Rueben Barwe's feature on the ZTV, 2012), as they jostled for positions, and even across parties involved in the liberation fight. After the death of Chitepo, Mugabe took over and gave up his secretary general position to another Manicaland leader, Edgar Tekere. Tekere was also a thorn in Mugabe's flesh later in 1990, with his Zimbabwe Unity Movement party (ZUM) that made a lot of noise in Zimbabwe's politics and elections.

During those late 1980s years, it also saw the rise of Arthur Mutambara, in student politics at the University of Zimbabwe, who created the legendary Zimbabwe student politics and strikes against the government of Mugabe. And then, in also came Morgan Tsvangirai, who is also a Manicaland son in the Zimbabwe Congress of Trade Union (ZCTU) politics as the secretary general of ZCTU. Tsvangirai and another Matabeleland son, Gibson Sibanda, authored the national strike protests against the government in the late 1990s, some of which resulted in those halcyon food riots of the late 1990s and managed the heart of the worker's political struggle. During the last election, in 2008, Tsvangirai with his party the MDC took over parliament from ZANUPF, and won the majority vote in the March presidential election. In these elections there were three leaders from Manicaland competing against Mugabe, that is, Tsvangirai, Mutambara, and Simba Makoni, and it is for this that Mugabe was angered by Manicaland people.

Manicaland people and Matabeleland people and their leaders have always felt alienated by the ruling Mashonaland (Zezuru), and Masvingo-Midlands (Karanga) ZANUPF leaders, so that people from Manicaland have always warmed up to its sons because it feels its sons have always been overlooked for the presidium in the ZANUPF. Even though it has produced leaders like Simba Makoni, Edgar Tekere, Maurice Nyagumbo, Movern Mahachi, Patrick Chinamasa, and Didymus Mutasa in the ZANUPF itself, of which none has made it to the presidium. The problem with the ZANUPF is that it doesn't really have leadership lines that it follows. After the death of Simon Muzenda, who was the first vice-president, that's when it became clear ZANUPF doesn't follow its own structures and leadership lines. I should think, Mutasa who was the Secretary of administration, or the Political Commissar, Mahachi, should have taken over, but both these Manicaland sons, including many other powerful politicians in the ZANUPF were overlooked as Mugabe choose Joyce Mujuru for this position. The rest of the party's structures had to endorse this, or incur the displeasure of Mugabe. This is where I even think a Matabeleland son, Joseph Msika, who was the second vice-president, should have been given this position. It should have been a political decision but they followed the 1987 unity accords. It is for some of these reasons that the Manicaland province has always rebelled against Mugabe, and was the first Shona rural province to accept Tsvangirai. It is now mostly controlled by the opposition.

The third most important region is Harare, Harare not just the city of Harare, but Harare as a province; this political province of Harare covers Seke rural, Chitungwiza city, Harare city, Ruwa town, Epworth, and the farming communities inside and surrounding these towns and cities. And, it is this province that usually has the final say on the political direction of the country, most of the times, single-handedly so, with far reaching consequences. Due to unregulated urban growth of the city and its surrounding areas, at the expense of all the other cities, it is by far bigger than its hinterlands such that most, if not all the people, end up coming to this city and its surrounding cities for employment and administrative functions. For example, for some years after independence, one could only apply for a passport in Harare. It had the only university for some years, several teachers and technical colleges, embassies, governments departments, foreign organisations, massive industries etc…, such that the total effect was it grew at the expense of its hinterlands. Even the second biggest urban city in this province, Chitungwiza, has been having an explosive population and residential properties growth. Just after independence, it was smaller than most of the other cities in the country, (Mutare, Gweru, and Bulawayo), in terms of residential area and population, but now, it is only second to Harare. Nowadays there is not even any concerted government policy to entice industries to invest in other cities, so that most of the investments are happening in Harare. This has made Harare very powerful, such that it decides most, if not the breath, of the country; politically, socially, etc...

The liberation war started way back in the 1960s and dragged for years without conclusion because it was being fought mostly outside the capital city. Smith and his government could have ill-afforded to continue fighting against the liberators, had the liberators stayed away from Harare, which was the sanctuary of most of the white people and Smith's government. But in the late 1970s, the liberation soldiers invaded Harare. I remember someday I was walking with a friend of mine, Augustine Nyakwangwa, in the Southerton industrial area of Harare, in the mid-1990s. We were passing by the BP Shell Company and we were told by the security and police who guarded the company to pass through on the other side of the road. It made me remember reading about how the liberation forces had bombed the BP Shell tanks during the war, and that, this had brought the country to its knees because of lack of fuel and forced Smith to negotiate sincerely and relinquish power. Harare hadn't suffered like all the other provinces had suffered from the liberation war, but by one stroke of an attack; Harare won the war for the whole country. Any leader in the State house would definitely scurry for cover, or be troubled if the capital is attacked. It simply means that even the leader could be attacked, as well.

During the Matabeleland uprising Harare was rather unconcerned and thus it didn't help Matabeleland in deciding Matabeleland's destiny. There were just minor skirmishes between the Ndebele and Shona people in this province. After all, the war was in the Matabeleland regions so Harare was unconcerned. The question is; did the people in Matabeleland wanted to take over Harare? I think not. They had neither the capacity nor ambition to do so. Maybe what they wanted, or were interested in, was to create a separate self-governing entity in the Matabeleland regions. Harare couldn't have helped them with that!

Harare started sizzling again in the late 80s and 90s with student politics and worker's strikes against the government. Morgan Tsvangirai managed to attract Harare's attentions and, in 1997-1999, Harare exploded in the violent strikes that brought the country to a halt and industry to its knees. Mugabe brought the soldiers and war amour into the streets of Harare, to quench off these dangerous strikes. The hottest spots were in Chitungwiza, Mbare and Highfields townships. These strikes and what they achieved galvanised

17

Tsvangirai, the labour, students, and activists to form the MDC, with Tsvangirai at the helm. This culminated in Harare voting overwhelmingly for the MDC and its partners, first in the No-vote to the constitution, and then in the elections in 2000. Ever since that Harare has always voted for the MDC, to the chagrin of ZANUPF and Mugabe. I remember the then information and publicity minister, Jonathan Moyo, who was also the spokesperson of the rejected constitution, drafted by the constitutional committee comprising some eminent judges, educationist and politicians (Judge Godfrey Chidyausiku, Judge Rita Makarau, Professor Walter Kamba and others. I will deal with the No-vote to the constitution later in the book), saying that, even though Tsvangirai had won all the seats in Harare he would not automatically lead the country because he had not won the majority vote nationwide. According to him, Harare is not Zimbabwe and Zimbabwe is not Harare. He was correct, but the Harareans couldn't help but laugh at this as another of Moyo's quips. These Harareans were joking, as well; by saying that Mugabe should relocate his State house and Munhumutapa offices to Uzumba-Maramba-Pfungwe since he had won that constituency overwhelmingly. Which is in Mashonaland east province, rather than staying in Harare where he was not liked, and thus slowly, Harare had started influencing the breath of the country again.

Another time Harare influenced the entire country was when the government, against better judgement, descended on Harare to punish it for rejecting ZANUPF in the previous elections, by rolling the graders, armoured soldiers' vehicles, the police, and the security operatives into the streets. Mostly it was in the high density townships: to destroy every illegal structure in these populous townships. I remember seeing the entourage of these vehicles passing us through in Seke road on our way to work. We wondered whether they had been another strike that we hadn't heard of, that morning in Chitungwiza, but when I arrived at my workplace, it was the talk from people from all over Harare's sprawling township suburbs. By mid-morning, news started filtering through of the destruction, of people's Boy's Skies (that's the name we gave to the illegal shacks or brick dwellings), illegal truck shops and illegal buildings; mostly in the high density areas where most of Harare's people stayed. Whole families were made shelter-less and slept outside in the winter's colds. Most of these people were informal traders, so without a home to stay in, without their workplaces which had also been destroyed, they were forced to leave for their rural homes, or to crash in with friends, or to disband out of the country altogether.

The aptly entitled Operation Murambatsvina was the government's ill-conceived idea to clean up Harare, and the rest of the countries' cities of dirty, but the political connotations behind this operation was that it was to clean up this cluster of the city's dissent against his rule. Why I say it was just a political decision; there was no single ministry that admitted this operation was under its jurisdiction? It seemed to be under Sekesai Makwavarara lead Harare commission, appointed by Ignatius Chombo, the minister of Local government, public works and urban development. This commission didn't even table this programme to the councillors of the city who were mostly from the MDC. Why was the operation only on-going in the cities, and why in the high density suburbs, and not throughout the whole city? They were a lot of illegal dwellings in the low density suburbs, even in the industries and the CBD which were left alone? There were powerful industrialists and politicians who had illegal buildings that never got destroyed in this drive. Why wasn't the operation applied throughout the country, even in the rural communities?

19

The government might have thought that through this operation they could destroy Harare's influence over the country, as political retribution, or it might be because they wanted to control political protest and future risk, or maybe to regain control of foreign currency dealings and support the 'Look East' policy. Little did the leadership at ZANUPF realised that they were precipitating Harare's influence, and helping spread Harare's influence directly into the rural areas they could still barely control? These people went back to their rural homes, not to preach to the villagers, of this government's leadership qualities, but what they had done to them, and how they had hurt and destroyed their careers, and lives.

There is a line a lot of people would draw when it comes to one's own flesh and blood. I wouldn't want to see my own kid hurting no matter whether he was wrong or right, and that's human nature. If the source of pain is something, or someone whom I have always supported, or admired, then there would be a sure change, in the support and admiration. Blood is thicker than water; I would turn my back against anyone who tries to hurt my kid unnecessarily or anyone I care about so deeply. This is the price that Mugabe paid for this insensitive clean-up, in the March 2008 election.

The young people he had made destitute in the clean-up became the rural area's activists, and that could be the reason why in the March elections (2008), Mugabe lost most of his rural support. He also even lost in a number of constituencies in his home province of Mashonaland west. This barbaric act also retched up pressure for Mugabe from the international community; by making the whole world to totally focus on Mugabe's human rights abuses, especially after the damning Anna Tibaijuka's drafted UN report, on this clean-up and the resulting refugee crisis it had created in Zimbabwe.

Excerpts of the report described the operation as disastrous and inhumane, representing a clear violation of International law. It affected directly, over 700 000 people, and indirectly it affected over 2.4 million people.

"The Operation has had a major economic, social, political and institutional impact on Zimbabwean society. The effects will be felt for many years to come, across all four dimensions. In social terms, the Operation has rendered people homeless and destitute, and created humanitarian and developmental needs that will require significant investment and assistance over several years. Economically, substantial housing stock has been destroyed, and the informal sector has virtually been wiped out, rendering individuals and households destitute. Local municipalities that used to collect taxes from informal traders have now lost this source of income. In political terms, the Operation has exacerbated an already tense and polarized climate characterized by mistrust and fear. It has resulted in a virtual breakdown in dialogue between Government and civil society. Institutionally, the Operation was conducted by central Government authorities, including the military, in an area that legally falls under the purview of local government." The report's executive summary stated.

This drive later on became known as Zimbabwe's Tsunami (in reference to the devastation which followed the tsunami caused by the 2005 Indian ocean earthquake), and or Operation Zvipwanyire Wega (destroy-it-yourself), after people took it over from the government and started doing the destruction themselves of their own illegal structures. If they waited for the government's destroyers

21

they could have lost other possessions like furniture and kitchen utensils in the government's utterly insensitive drive. The government drive didn't care what was inside those structures. The graders just struck the structures and a number of people had died in this government's drive, so to be on the safe side, you had to destroy it yourself.

This international pressure resultant of this operation culminated in countries like the UK, USA, Australia, EU, Canada, New Zealand, and Japan tightening the screws on Mugabe and his cronies. They applied and broadened the sanctions. These countries also made more funds available for the democratic struggles and human rights fighters. The United states had since drafted and passed into law the Zimbabwe Democracy and Economic Recovery Act(2001), and was channelling funds to opposition activists through this mechanism, whilst the United kingdom used its Westminster Fund to channel money to the opposition, so did many western nations, through various institutions, NGOs, charities, donor organisations. Zimbabwe really entered into international focus, and people in far-flung countries, who in the first place, hadn't cared that much about their governments' obsession with the Zimbabwean issue started taking interest especially after they saw, on their own national televisions, like the CNN, BBC, and CFI, what Mugabe had done to innocent civilians. They started putting pressure on their own leaders to rein in Mugabe against human rights abuses.

All through the previous election years Mugabe had always descended into the rural areas and closed them of from the opposition and the international media. Whatever stories that managed to come out of political killings were not substantiated because nobody knew what was really happening out there. Mugabe would always bully this rural vote, and ultimately win the national vote and; his coterie of apologist like the SADC, AU, would always declare those elections as free and fair, thereby staying Mugabe from international rejection. Since they didn't have real time evidence, of political abuses, the international community could only come to terms with SADC and AU decisions of the 2000, 2002, 2005 elections. In the June 2008 elections ZANUPF made another blunder when they used their perfected methods on Harare's electorate and tried to close Harare of, by throwing the youths and militias onto Harare. They were trying to displace Tsvangirai's support in this area. As usual, they also closed the rural areas.

For the first time ZANUPF's electioning methods came into spotlight because Harare has always been covered well by the international media organisations. All that was happening was being broadcast directly to the outside world. Due to the spreading usage of satellite broadcasting and internet communication in this province, everyone became aware of what was really happening in Zimbabwe, not the fodder that we were getting from ZANUPF controlled broadcaster, the ZBC. Ordinary people became the real journalists, and like eye-witness news, they would record the event and broadcast it on the internet, or sent it through as text messages on their cell phones. Instantly, the information would become available to the breath of the country and the whole world. A lot of people had also stopped watching the ZBC fodder, and this resulted in the increase of illegal satellite dishes and broadcasting, all over the cities; as people resorted to any free news channels on this satellite broadcasting, like France 24, SABC, etv, BTV etc... This eye witness news gathering method was adopted by most of the international Medias who had been denied entry into Zimbabwe. Thus the international community focused on Harare.

Even at that, SADC and AU observers also became aware, and were ashamed of ZANUPF's election dirty tactics, when they themselves where beaten up by the police, security operatives, and the army when they tried to cover Tsvangirai's election rally at the Showground (Glamis stadium). Nobody in his right senses would have ignored that and declared the elections as free and fair. For the first time these observers declared the elections as unfair. Once again Harare had sizzled and decided the fate of Zimbabwe's political dispensation. Had Mugabe stayed away from Harare, especially Tsvangirai's last rally, we could have been talking of a different story, on the outcome of the June 2008 poll.

Farm Invasion Episode

" An 8 year old Zimbabwean girl has been mauled by two lions that were supposed to protect her from war veterans intent on claiming her family's farm" The Star, 29 September 2008. An earlier Rapport newspaper report had stated that one of the lions had spotted Courtney Sparrow through a window and dragged her out of the house. The lions had been secured in front of the house after surviving the farm's fourth war veteran attack in three months, during which Courtney's mother had single-handedly chased away the invaders with a firearm.

I know there are a lot of people out there who are saying, "Oh please! What were the lions doing at a farm, with civilised people, not even in the Zoo at that!" Some are even dismissing this story into Tarzanesque movies. Some have a lot of questions; some are even deriding the journalists who wrote about this story. Some are asking why I have started with this "outlandish" story. I am dealing with an "outlandish" issue. I mean the way the land reform was carried out in Zimbabwe was outlandishly, to say the least. Cathy Buckle in her two books, *African Tears*, and *Beyond African Tears*, records some of these outlandish ways in which it happened. She also wrote emails during that period which are available on the internet. There are many other writers who have covered this issue. I am not going to write the whole book focussing on the land issue alone so I am not going to cover it in minute particulars. My angle is on whether the land reform, or invasion or whatever that happened in Zimbabwe, and the ensuing madness, is still on-going. The next angle is on whether the land issue was really important at that time for the country when it happened. Is that what the Zimbabweans wanted, or the majority Zimbabweans, or even at that, the black majority really wanted?

The above newspaper story reminded me of a century or so ago, I mean the way the white man, we are told, was given the land. In his often repeated speech on the television, i.e. ZTV, Herbert Chitepo (deceased former ZANU leader), is heard saying the whites pegged their land using a horse. The first day the white man would ride it until it was tired to the northern direction and peg the point, the morrow day he would ride it to the east and do the same, then he would do the southern direction the next day, and complete with the westerly direction, thus pegging the boundaries of his farm. Some land, Chitepo said, was paid for a shilling an acre. On top of that, the black people who owned that land were told they were now squatters, would instantly be paying land tax to a white owner for staying on his land; or work for the white man to pay for their stay there. Most of this tax was paid through confiscation of the husbandry of the black person, thus ultimately pushing the black person off his land.

Over a century later, the black man concocted their own revenge. The stories we heard during the farm invasion times were outlandish, like the above story. The above quoted newspaper story happened under a backdrop in which Mugabe, in the same breathe was denying that farm invasions were still continuing, and then say; they were still continuing and would never end. Call them land redistribution, or farm invasion, it's the same process and the same outcome. This land issue reached new heights, when it was epitomized by the violent takeover of Alamein Farm by the retired Army General, Solomon Mujuru, which sparked the first legal action against one of Robert

26

Mugabe's inner circle.

In late 2002, the seizure was ruled illegal by the High and Supreme Courts of Zimbabwe, however the previous owner was unable to effect the court orders and Mujuru continued living at the farm until his death on 15 August 2011. Farms like Kondozi Farm were taken, re-taken, invaded, re-invaded by the breath of the ZANUPF leadership, down to the war veterans and became a war zone, of ZANUPF power struggles until the government decided to give it to ARDA(Agricultural Research and Development Authority). It just took them very little time to run it to the ground.

It is the same company that trained our inept agricultural minister, Joseph Made. It's no wonder the agricultural sector in Zimbabwe during Made's tenure has been ridiculed. Just like what Mugabe was doing with the farm issue (the contrasting answers whether the land invasions were still on-going or not), Made, in the same breathe would tell you that the country has enough food to feed its people until the next coming farming season, and then admits that the country would need to import some more food, and then lies that the country has made all contingency plans to secure the food to supplement the deficit. But don't take it at that face-value because down the line he will excuse the shortages on non-availability of foreign currency and a whole other reason as the country staved.

Some time, end of 2003, we went to sell some wares in Concession area with my friend, Joseph Mugore. Concession is in the Mashonaland Central province. We had tobacco cigarettes, wines and spirits which we were trading. There was this illegal mining happening deep in the commercial farming communities of Concession, at a place known as Mushazhike. These illegal miners

27

were mining gold in this area. We were part of the hordes that were providing trade to these people who were far removed from the nearest trading centre. People brought basic commodities for trade, and these illegal panniers sold their gold to illegal gold dealers who were also there. At the time we were there, for about 5 days, there were a total of 5000 plus traders who passed through that place; who also included the policeman whom we played hide and seek with as they tried to arrest us for this illegal business. If you got caught all that you had to do was bribe those policemen off. The whole place had been desecrated and barren crates, holes, dilapidated shacks were all over this place, and the stream had been flooded by sand, and sometimes blocked. The land that should have been used for crop and cattle farming had been consumed by these illegal activities. The farm next to where we were had been occupied by one of the notorious war veterans leader, Jabulani Sibanda, who had been one of the prime movers of the farm invasion programme in Zimbabwe.

After selling our wares, my friend and I decided to walk to the next shopping centre, which was near Mazowe town, and near where we were than was Concession, in a bid to save on the little we made from our endeavours by foregoing transport fares to Concession, which was very expensive. The shopping centre is known as Jumbo shopping centre where we took taxis to Mazowe. It is a distance of nearly10km from Mushazhike, and we walked through prime farmlands. The sad thing was that not even a single farm had been cultivated for farming that year, yet it was already in December, mid farming season and it was raining well that year. We had to even deal with a huge storm the time we were there. I wrote a story on that entitled, Mushazhike, which is part of a novel of interlinked short stories entitled, Notes from a Modern Chimurenga. I am not going to delve into the emotionality of this journey, the struggles, and the difficulty of that endeavour in this writing.

Mushazhike area has one of the finest soils in Zimbabwe; black, grey, red clay soils which are so rich in nutrients such that one wouldn't have to put a lot of artificial fertilizers for the crops. And yet, not even a single farm had been cultivated, not even this popular war veteran's farm. This reinforced the feeling that I had developed about the land reform programme, all along. Before that, I had seen some prime tobacco farms along Chitungwiza and Seke road, between Harare and Chitungwiza, being reduced into redundant land by the new farmers, who could only use those farms to grow maize and Soya beans. These crops were not suitable for this land. The crops never matured due to water logging and lack of fertilizers. Nowadays, if you travel through any road out of Harare into the rural communities, all that you can see are vast tracts of farm lands abandoned, misused, and mismanaged by these so called new farmers. It's no wonder that Zimbabwe has had to import food ever since the farm invasions in year 2000.

In a related survey conducted by Ian Soones (2011), of The Institute of Development Studies, University of Sussex, UK, he says rough official figures state that in about 7.6 million hectares or about 20per cent Zimbabwe's area redistributed since 2000, Crops for export such as tobacco, coffee and tea have suffered the most under the land reform, with e.g. a reduction in tobacco production by 43per cent from 2000 to 2009. According to this 10-year survey of 400 households located in Masvingo province, he also says the main every-day food for Zimbabweans, maize, has been reduced by 31per cent, while small grains production has grown by 163per cent. He also said that the Government's racially motivated seizures of white-

29

owned lands, and the re-distribution of much of these lands to ZANU-PF party officials, is still continuing. As of 2011, that there are now fewer than 300 white farmers (from 4 000 before farm invasions) remaining in Zimbabwe.

It's not that I disagree with the land reform entirely, no; if land had to be distributed, it had to be done in a planned, legally binding, and constructive way. I believe people who really deserved to get land for commercial purposes, people who knew how to farm this land like trained experts from colleges, universities and even trained farm workers, had to get the land. I also feel an environment conducive for these new breed of farmers had to be created before land was distributed.

I also believe that the commercial white farmers were to blame for refusing, or frustrating the government's efforts to acquire land over the years. In 1992, the Land Acquisition Act was enacted to speed up the land reform process by removing the "willing seller, willing buyer" clause (of the Lancaster house agreements provisions), also limiting the size of farms and introducing a land tax (although the tax was never implemented.) The Act empowered the government to buy land compulsorily for redistribution, and a fair compensation was to be paid for land acquired. But the Landowners could challenge in court the price set by the acquiring authority. Thus, opposition by landowners increased throughout the period before the forced Fast track land reform, in year 2000. The commercial farmers could go to the extent of tangling the government in court battles over the acquisition process, and most of the times, they made available to the government land that was not good for farming; or even cattle grazing. Some white farmers had vast tracts of land which they were not even using but still refused with it. Some of these unutilised vast tracts of land were owned by single families who were no longer, or have never stayed in Zimbabwe, or were not Zimbabwe's citizens like the Openheimers. These people were protected by the government's bilateral trade protocols and this land was left idle. But the way the government embarked on this land reform was, to be very moderate, totally wrong.

These farm invaders were allowed and protected, by the government, to compulsorily occupy every farm they could, and did so like a country at war with its "other" citizens. There were killings, beatings, raping, etc… of White farmers or Black farm workers (Smith, Steven and others were killed in the Macheke-Marondera farming communities). These occupiers, with open government support, disrupted everything, occupied almost all the farms, whether the farm was being utilised or not, whether it was too large or not, whether it was a commercial estate or safari or not, whether it had crops in it or not. They butchered herds of animals and husbandry for their own consumption or to sell, burned tobacco burns with tobacco in it etc... They copied the white man's prototype of over a century before and ransacked the white farming communities and grabbed everything they could from the scurrying white farmers.

Sometime before this land grab, in September 1998, there was a land conference that was carried out between Britain (and the other donors) and the Zimbabwean government in which the government had been promised funds by the USA and UK governments to continue with acquisition of land on a willing buyer willing seller basis, which, even though at that time, had expired. Forty-eight countries and international organizations attended and unanimously endorsed the land program, saying it was essential for poverty reduction, political stability and economic growth. They agreed that

31

the inception phase, covering the first 24 months, should start immediately, particularly appreciating the political imperative and urgency of the proposal. The Commercial Farmers Union (CFU) also tabled over 50 000 hectares that government could acquire straight away.

The government was promised funds to pay the white farmers, for improvements done on the farms, and for the developmental needs of the new resettled farmers, and the farming communities. The government had agreed to that, but it seems; after being defeated in the Constitutional Referendum (in the No-vote to the constitution) in February 2000, the government broke these gentlemen's agreements. They allowed the war veterans to occupy the white commercial farmer's land, whom ZANUPF also accused of having supported and financed the No-vote against the constitutional referendum. This group of war veterans also included clusters of the dreaded C.I.O, the police, the army, and ZANUPF youths. Those who invaded these farms were mostly ZANUPF members. The idea could have been to extrude the whites out of the farms, or to extinguish them, altogether.

There is this trait that has come to light about Mugabe, that is, in Mugabe's world there is no forgiveness or real reconciliation. If he feels that you have done him a wrong, or even a perceived wrong, some day he would make you pay. Like the Matebeleland people who were made to pay for, especially, the sins or mistakes of their leaders, of going against him after the liberation struggle; even for the fact that Matebeleland region had never been interested in him and was an unavailable-to-him part of Zimbabwe. Also every opposition member against his rule, all and sundry, have been treated savagely. Some have been jailed, beaten up, or even be brought before the courts for cooked up charges. Ndabaningi Sithole, Morgan

32

Tsvangirai, and many others have felt the ugly side of Mugabe's anger. In this case, it was the white farmers who were being made to pay for the sins of their fathers. For all that, it makes me feel Mugabe must be a rabid racist. He is always disparaging the white part of our population, even for concocted wrongs they never did. I think he doesn't want them to have anything to do with the country's governance, just because they are white. In his mind, whiteness doesn't have to equate with Africanness. And there are only two ways Mugabe makes you pay, that is extinguishing you, or extruding you out.

At that time, another group of those war veterans were also thrown on any opposition against Mugabe's rule, like civic organisations, Trade unions, the Judiciary and all other institutions perceived to be at loggerheads with this government. At about that time everyone was running and stampeding out of or around the country. It created total anarchy and within this chaotic situation, the ZANUPF deceived the people into voting for them using the land reform as a tramp card.

It is not that people were in dire need of land, I mean the biggest part of the Zimbabweans were not in need of land. A lot of people never thought of farming as a career option, not a lot of those who grew up in post-independence Zimbabwe, who now constituted the biggest majority in Zimbabwe. The guys I grew up with never had farming as a career option. It was people who were older, who were more in tune with this programme, who also wanted to have a little piece of land to partly farm and build a home on. Mugabe knew that the land issue will relate with the older part of our population for it is for this that the liberation struggle was also fought for. To them, freedom comes through possession of land. That could be the reason why

33

after so many years of independence, and even when things became more and more difficult, economically difficult for the entire country, this older group of the population always voted for Mugabe. Even the 43per cent Mugabe got in the March 2008 election must have come from this old-age group.

I remember during these previous elections, and especially in the June 2008 election, getting into a fierce argument with an elderly neighbour who was in her 70's. She had to travel by foot, from her small farm in the Beatrice area to Zengeza Township, in Chitungwiza city, a day before the elections so that she could vote in her registered ward, Ward 7. She had to make this distance of about 60 km just to vote for Mugabe, she said, who had given her land. The argument came about when she asked for money for transport back to the farm from me. I was angry with her because instead of helping us- young people- by voting Mugabe out, rather she was helping him to stay. Like salt on the wound, she wanted me to help finance her and help her destroy this dream some of us had of removing Mugabe. I later on gave her the money anyway, because, despite everything, she had been a good friend over the years. I looked up to her as my grandmother, helping me when I was in need.

In late 2007, Gideon Gono, the Reserve Bank governor, printed a lot of money, in trillions and trillions of dollars. He invaded the motor industry where I was working, in a sales office of one of the major motor vehicle sales dealerships in Zimbabwe. Every sale of motor vehicles was being made to the Reserve Bank, in those days, in all the established dealerships in Harare. Even production at Willowvale Mazda Motor Industries was stopped for everyone else, for some time, but for the Reserve Bank. These vehicles were touted to be used for the Reserve Bank's second "Operation Sunrise programme", but later on, ended up in the hands of the election campaign machine, for the 2008 election. At the same time, Gono also invaded most of the companies that manufactured agricultural equipments and inputs. Particularly, I remember my cousin telling me that the company he worked for, a subsidiary of SIRDC (Scientific Industrial Research and Development Cooperation), a government company, had also been given a huge order to manufacture agricultural equipments for the coming 2008 agricultural season. The government, through the Reserve Bank, also bought a lot of fuel, fertilizers, combine harvesters, and tractors by using foreign currency it compulsorily took from FCA accounts of private individuals and institutions without their knowledge. There was a furore when it was even brought into light that they took money that was set aside for HIV, AIDS patients for these endeavours.

The government's intent was to capacitate this new farming community created by the farm invasions and land redistribution. As I have already said, not a single one of those endeavours had been financed well, and none had been fully paid for by the government. Most of these agricultural equipments and inputs were given to ZANUPF bigwigs. Gono himself and a cluster of war veterans got some of this largesse. The majority of ordinary farmers were given a couple or so of substandard implements, fertilizers, and seed packs of Maize and Soya bean seeds.

Whilst the whole country was struggling to find fuel to fuel the industry, these farmers were given abundant fuel to use for planting their farms. Instead of using the fuel for the said purposes, they rather diverted it to the black market, even at exorbitant prices, and or either rented out the equipment, or sold them outrightly. So also was seed Maize and Soya beans seeds sold on the black market. You

35

could go to Mbare and Chikwanha markets and get all the farming things that you would need on the black-market there, yet they were not available in agric-shops where they should have been available, at reasonable prices. Here is the idea I am trying to put across. The Government had to print money and even took people's foreign currency to buy these things, at exorbitant prices, from their favoured manufacturers who were either government parastatals or ZANUPF bigwigs companies. All this was done to capacitate new farmers but these new farmers who were given these things sold them at the black market, at exorbitant prices, thereby fuelling the black market prices and inflation. The farms were left uncultivated by these new farmers so nothing productive came out from this endeavour.

To these new farmers; it was why waste time in farming crops that would ultimately be sold at controlled, low prices to the Grain Marketing Board when they could just sell whatever equipment and inputs, including the fuel, at prices that they would never dream of fetching by using those things for farming. Why wait for an entire farming season, why tempt fate?

I have a friend, and have been friends with for years. He was part of the first wave of farm invaders, the first war veterans who invaded farms in the Beatrice area, just outside Harare. Over the years, I have always had an opportunity to talk to him for we also stayed in the same street. This friend was born in 1979, in Harare, but he also posed as a war veteran when that madness started. I used to tease him about what kind of war he had fought in his mother's womb, for him to qualify for war veteran status. When he was born the war was over then. He also benefited from these overtures from the Reserve Bank. He also had a piece of land in the Beatrice area, but all that I have known; he never produced anything from his farm. Every planting season he got his full share of implements and inputs which he always sold at the black market. He always would disappear from the streets, about the beginning of the planting season for his plot. By about the middle of the season, he will be back in the streets with a little bit of money to spent. I used to call him a political prostitute for he had joined every of the three major parties in Zimbabwe, only to benefit from whatever he would be given by the party he will be involved with at that time.

During the March 2008 election he was now campaigning with the new kid on the block, Arthur Mutambara, who was vying for the Zengeza West constituency. He was also vying for a ward in the Zengeza 2 area, as a councillor. At one time they did a door to door campaign in Zengeza 2, in his ward, with Mutambara. They were both defeated in the elections by their competitors in this area.

Talking to him about Zimbabwe's politics and the land reform programme was an insane exercise. It was like trying to figure out the complexities of Zimbabwe's history and its general politics. He would go around, around in circles, disappear and re-appear, die and rise from the dead, with his political ideologies. Like the complexities of his ideologies, so was the complexities of the land invasions where it was so difficult to single out a good thing that came out of it to write home about.

Some many moons ago, in the 80s, when were boys, my two uncles whom we had stayed with, left our communal lands in Mapfurira, Nyatate, in the Nyanga district, to the resettlement areas around us. The oldest one went to Magaya farm, i.e. village 1, and the youngest to Ziwa farm, i.e. village 4. They were part of the people that got farming land after independence. Over the years we have also kept in touch with all those who had left for the resettlement farms nearby. They were still within walking distance, in the former white farms areas, around Nyatate. Over the years, there was this farming competition done every year in and around Nyatate area; whereby one farmer was chosen as the best farmer for that year. He was given some goodies which comprised, mostly of agric inputs and equipments to use for the next farming season. My mother was the secretary of the Agricultural Cooperative Society for the whole of the Nyatate area. This was the organisation which organised this programme, and every aspect of farming, like sourcing of the inputs and dissemination of agricultural training, seminars, and competitions like the above mentioned, "Master Farmer competition", field days, collecting and transporting agriculture outputs for the whole area and organising and liaising with the Grain Marketing Board to transport produce to its Silos in Nyanga town. It was a volunteer, unpaid job that took a lot of my mother's time. We had to chip in a lot to help her, in farming our own plots, over 25 acres, even in some of those Cooperative activities; such that we grew up knowing most of the information on farming and farming activities in this area.

The best farmers came from the former communal farming areas of Nyatate. Few came from these new resettlement areas. Most of the field days were subsequently held in the communal areas. Both my Uncles never did better than us. We were always one of the best farmers of this area, season-in season-out, even though we were still farming the same communal (Tribal Trust Lands). You could count just a few farmers who did better than us in the new resettlement areas. The rest, of these resettled farmers, were non-performers for some time, and could only keep to their jobs in the cities and use the farms to build homes. Quite a lot of them survived by buying food from us; people who had stayed behind in the tribal trust lands.

During this period 1980-1990, it is when most of Zimbabwe's resettlement happened. This was a well-financed endeavour, by the western donors and the British government (over 44 million pounds invested in the land acquisition, and over 500 million pounds for budgets surplus which also might have included land acquisitions). It is this period that Zimbabwe became known as the "bread basket" of Africa, exporting its excess all over Africa. It still maintained this proud mantle through to the mid 1990's; especially with the help we got from the donor community. And then, by about the middle 1990s, the Lancaster agreement provisions had since expired in 1990, but we still were getting funding from Britain.

I want to regress a bit on the Lancaster house agreements. The UK government still refuse to acknowledge the often repeated assertion that it had agreed, during the negotiations, that it would be bound into financing, or paying compensation money for the land issue. On 5 November 1997, Britain's then secretary of state for international development, Claire Short, described the new Labour government's approach to the Zimbabwean land reform, that the government was not bound by the colonial agreements or injustices, since her government comprised of people from say, Ireland, where her ancestors came from, who never colonized Africa, and were at that, colonized by Britain herself during that time. Notwithstanding this petulant assertion, and the Lancaster House commitments, Short also stated that her government was only prepared to support a programme of land reform that was part of a poverty eradication strategy. She had other questions regarding the way in which land would be acquired and compensation paid, and the transparency of the whole process. Britain always says it only agreed to do the financing of land acquisitions and development later, after

39

independence, by meeting 50per cent of the costs of land purchase and of the investments (water, schools, clinics, etc.) required to convert large commercial farms into viable resettlement areas for peasant or communal farming. Around 71,000 families (perhaps over 500,000 people) settled on 3.5 million hectares of former white-owned land under this programme, which was described by "The Economist" in 1989 as "perhaps the most successful aid programme in Africa".

In 2007, the Secretary-General of the Commonwealth at the time of the Agreement, Sir Shridath Ramphal, spoke out for the first time about a secret deal saying, "I took an initiative of my own as Secretary-General which isn't much known and talked about but can be now." Sir Shridath confirmed that in the face of collapse of Agreement talks (over the land issues) and with the potential for reversing into civil war, he secretly contacted the US ambassador in London, Kingman Brewster, and asked him to get the then US President, Jimmy Carter, to promise money to pay white farmers for their land. He quickly received assurances authorized by the American President, 'that the United States would contribute a substantial amount for a process of land redistribution and they would undertake to encourage the British government to give similar assurances'. Even the "Declaration of Rights" that forms part of the Agreement and was entrenched in the constitution for ten years included a carefully worded section allowing the compulsory purchase of under-occupied land for settlement purposes, balanced by clauses requiring payment of compensation that could be remitted overseas. This clause was never used by the Zimbabwe government. The issue of British aid for land reform was not discussed at Lancaster House. Although the Patriotic Front (ZANU and ZAPU) representatives claimed to have received satisfactory assurances, no evidence of any secret deal is available, other than the one stated above.

Enough of this historicity, but what I am trying to get at is that through this working together we were still feeding our people; and exporting in excess as a nation. A difference was being made in the resettlement areas where production was increasing, through this help and working together with our donors. As a country we should have continued in this spirit, slowly taking over from the white community and the white community and donors helping us doing that until such a time when land was equitably owned in Zimbabwe, without having to go through what we had to go through. Civilisations don't happen in a day. Rome was not built in a day. Even Barrack Obama; a black president in America, was an unthinkable thing in some few decades ago.

The mercenary attitude taken by the war veterans, or even the former liberation fighters was untenable. They should have understood that when they fought for freedom, or land, they were not fighting for themselves and their families but for the rest of the country. That's the meaning of patriotism. Only mercenaries go to a war expecting only them to benefit from the war.

But the truth is, and if it has to be repeated, there was no dire need of land in Zimbabwe. A lot of us were still trying to come to terms with the land we had by farming it commercially. If you look at my family particularly, and many others in my rural village, and though my father and mother are still into farming, all the children in our family have left home for the cities and none of us would like to go back and stay in the rural areas and be a farmer. We grew up there; farming and we understand, is not an easy career to pursue. There is a lot of work involved and risks.

Nowadays, my parents no longer utilise all the land we have like we used to do when we were growing up. A lot of the land is lying unutilised in the communal lands, worst still in the old resettlement areas because most of the children who did most of the work have left for the cities. Even most, if not all, of my cousins are out in the towns, or outside the country. This other day I asked for and tried to trace the guys I grew up with in Nyatate. I found out that half of the guys were now staying in South Africa alone. I bet none would be thinking of returning back to Zimbabwe to be farmers. I suppose, quite a number, would return at a heartbeat if industry and services were to return to their early 1990's levels, but definitely not for farming. A lot would even prefer to move further afield- abroad- to experience life in other countries. Such is the effect of the global village!

Mugabe's generation, especially the war veterans took the wishes of the whole country for granted and went on to impose their kind of destiny, they wanted on the entire country and on all the other generations. Here, he should have weighed the pros and cons of this forced takeover of the farms. He should have realised there were going to be ructions against this. As a reaction to the fast-track land reform the United States government put the Zimbabwean government on a credit freeze in 2001 through the Zimbabwe Democracy and Economic Recovery Act of 2001(specifically Section 4C titled Multilateral Financing Restriction). This collapsed the trade surplus in 2002. Where there was a trade surplus of $322 million in 2001, in 2002 the credit freeze led to a trade deficit of $18 million, to grow rapidly in subsequent years. In farming, mostly crops for export

42

suffered severely, e.g. Zimbabwe was the world's 6th largest producer of Tobacco in 2001, it produces nowadays less than 1/3 of the amount produced in 2000; the lowest amount in 50 years. Zimbabwe was also once so rich in agricultural produce that it was dubbed the "bread basket" of Southern Africa, whilst now it is struggling to feed its own population. About 45 per cent of the population is considered malnourished. Other studies also ascertain that the Zimbabweans are now living a far poorer life, than say, pre-1953 levels.

I will have to repeat it again; that it's not land that we wanted from our government. My generation, and even people younger than me, could have done better with a lot more freedom, both political and economic, better social services from the government like better hospitals, better health delivery, better schools, better infrastructure, better education, better skills development and enlightenment, better technology and communication, better jobs, better industries-manufacturing and services- better labour laws. But because of this land madness we had to forgo all that, just for some few farms which were given to the few generality of Zimbabwe who wanted the land. I would have to judge Mugabe on this. This makes me rewind back to a time at the height of the farm invasions.

There was also a friend of mine, from that time, Nyundo yeZimbabwe, that was his Chimurenga name, so we simply called him Nyundo. He spearheaded farm invasion in the Beatrice area, and during that time when he came back into the street, we would argue; sometimes so fiercely, about this programme. Even in times when he couldn't find me at home he would make sure he returns back and search around for me, until he finds me to argue his case out. He was one older person I didn't care to hurt by just saying what I wanted to say. He took it exceptionally well, and that way, we became very good friends even though we differed so fiercely on the land issue. He was around 48 years old and I was in my late 20's then, but we clicked by agreeing to differ. Yet, there were instances I saw how this farm issue had torn apart Zimbabwe's human fabric. One day we had been arguing so fiercely. We were talking of the killings of the white farmers in Macheke area. I was saying as a people we had gone too far. That the war veterans had twisted every good intention of the land reform, and had made it seem like the country had gone to war against its 'other' citizens. He was saying it was necessary, since to them, it was now war-time. They didn't care what the majority population of Zimbabwe thought. It was their right to curve out this destiny for the whole country. It's them who had liberated us from the colonisers whom he felt we now had a soft spot for.

Out of anger, I told him that we could have liberated the country, as well, had we been older. That they should return it back to the colonisers and see whether we would not be able to liberate it. That, just because they were on the forefront of the liberation war, it doesn't mean that we didn't contribute, through for instance housing them and giving them food to eat. That they were behaving like mercenaries, who always expect to be compensated for every good or bad they had done. I told him to stop thinking that they did this alone and take the country to ransom over it. He was so angry with me, and at that time, I was so scared he would beat me. He said that the next thing there were going to do was to take one of those white farmers into First Street, in Harare city centre. Cut him into pieces and then roast his pieces and eat them in the full glare of the foreign media, the leadership, and the entire country for everyone else in Zimbabwe to take them seriously on this issue. I knew they wouldn't do that, and even though I fought him that day, all the way; deep down I was troubled with what he had said. Thinking about all that now makes me realise the depth with which we had sunk so low as a country, and how we have stayed that low ever since.

I will go back to what had inspired this piece of writing, in the first place.

Is farm invasion still continuing?

Commercial Farmers Union, which mainly represents the white commercial farmers, said the attacks by the militants, from Mugabe's ZANUPF had increased over the last month (January 2009), and urged the new government to take action saying. "As of yesterday (25 February 2009), we had 77 incidents. We don't see any change with the Unity Government" CFU chief executive, Hendrik Olivier said. Tsvangirai, now the prime minister, denounced the attacks, saying the violence was undermining efforts to revive the shattered farm sector, which was once the backbone of the economy.

"I have asked the ministers of home affairs to bring the full weight of the law down on the perpetrators who continue to act within a culture of impunity. No person in Zimbabwe is above the law."

Unless things have miraculously changed, I believe Tsvangirai should know better, that it is exactly the opposite of what he said that obtains in Zimbabwe, Unity Government, or no Unity Government. The culture of Impunity has been the catch phrase from the farm invasions of year 2000, up to post-power sharing agreements. Until such a time when he will be in control of the security apparatus in Zimbabwe, until they respect him as a genuine representative of some Zimbabweans' viewpoint, then he will be able to say something that the militants would listen to. For starters, Tsvangirai should demand that the security sector leaders, Chiwenga, Chihuri, Shiri, Sibanda, and Zimhondi, respect him. I don't mean to salute him; I mean to respect his views as part of Zimbabwe's views. If they can do that, it also means their wayward elements (militants) in the security structures would take a leaf, and start the process of recognising his authority. Without that, I feel the farms will never be safe, and this culture of impunity won't change much in this new Unity Government arrangement, not only just in the farms but throughout all the facets of governance in the country.

Is farm invasion still continuing?

Yes it is.

As long as those who invaded farms illegally are still staying on those farms, illegally, then it's just as good to say that farm invasions are still on-going. And yes, there are still there on the farms; illegally.

Undated Journals: Two Weeks Before 27 June 2008.

In the first election in March 2008 Tsvangirai had defeated Mugabe by 47per cent against 43per cent, so there had to be a run-off since nobody had got the constitutionally 50 per cent plus one vote needed... some politicians tricked the country into thinking what was needed was 51 percent?

Mugabe and his campaign machine are doing sharp. They are preaching for this 51per cent idea, sharper like a magpie. The whole country seems to have bought into this. These seem to be the rules... There are no basic commodities in the shops, but at the black market with prices so exorbitantly high. There are queues all over the country. In a story that happened, a certain man finds people queuing and joins the queue without even asking what the queue was for. It is a very long queue but he follows it through. When he gets to the front he realises that people have not been queuing for food items as he had supposed they were on the queue for. They were on this queue to get blessed by an apostolic faith healer. He is an atheist so he curses himself as he abandons this queue. People had been acculturated to the idea that things have to be queued for. "The only thing for free, without having to queue for, is sunshine and air", people would ruefully joke at each other.

Most social institutions are down, and social services are non-existent. You can only be able to use electricity for cooking once in 2 to 3 weeks because most of the times, it is out. When electricity comes on, people would celebrate in the streets, as if celebrating for the second coming of the Messiah. Fuel is on the black market only. It changes prices 3 times per day so there is no fuel to be lit. Fuel is unbelievably out of reach of the general people in the streets, so that people are depending on firewood for cooking, or even plastics, grass, and rubbish materials from the dumping grounds, all over the streets, to cook Sadza (a thickened pasty porridge cooked using Maize meal flour) that would ultimately be so smelly from the fumes. But we eat it nevertheless; drink some water and go to sleep.

Chitungwiza is now a waterway as several sewer pipes are bursting, dumping smelly sewage shit all over the streets. Little kids play in these river sewages we have to jump over as we carry about on whatever business of life we are up to. The place is so smelly; you would almost think there is no need of using the toilets. Why not just do it the old cave age way, right there in the middle of the streets.

There is no foreign currency, other than on the black market, at inflated prices. Transport fares have skyrocketed such that the money we would get from our workplaces won't run beyond a week, or so, after payday. I have since resigned at my workplace, in March, so have done a lot of people, as they leave for greener pastures. I would be going back to South Africa. I have come to process my travel documents. There is no longer any financial gain in going to work for a lot of us. The highest Zimbabwean dollar note can't buy a loaf of bread and do you know how much it is? $100 billion, and if we add back the three zeroes cut by Gono, it should be $100 trillion. Some people are earning this bill for a month's salary, at their workplaces. They are supposed to make ends-meat, with this bill, until month's end.

Schools are being closed, opened, closed, opened... with teacher's shortages, strikes, the government's bungling of the education system, elections and elections, and conversion of these schools into military barracks and political bases. During this electioning period people are being forced to go to these military and political bases, every night. They would spend the entire night singing revolutionary songs at these bases. If you refuse to go you would be beaten to death. Laws to suppress the people are still being thrown, here and there, and the next moment they are ignored. All this is being done to protect the leaders here.

*****

I am thinking that these things won't last, like shutting eyes, like dreams we had so many years ago, but they last. It is on the 14th of June that they invade our little township, Zengeza Township. They come early in the morning loaded to the full with ZANUPF's party regalia, and weapons. The riot police are there, as are there too; the army and security operatives. Chances to meet them becomes street-chances so nobody is safe from them. Indigenous business people who sell their wares at the Flee market at Zengeza 2 shopping centre have been told to evacuate from the premises they have always paid rent for. These indigenous business people include those who sell vegetables, tomatoes, small tools, and foreign currency exchange dealers. They have been told to evacuate these premises by Council leaders, in connivance with ZANUPF leaders, the Riot police, Army, ZANUPF militias, and some rogue former MDC members who had joined ZANUPF, in order to benefit from this clean-up campaign. There are no election observers around. I have never seen them around here, anyway. After all, there are just a few of them so I don't expect them to witness this.

These small business people were being accused of supporting and voting for the MDC, in the previous March elections. These people were told to stop their support of the MDC, to buy ZANUPF cards, and attend ZANUPF rallies in which they would denounce MDC. Then they would be accordingly embraced into ZANUPF party. A lot of them ended up doing that but their wares had already been confiscated. Some wares rot and a lot of business is lost. All of a sudden, they become beggars for survival. I pass through this now deserted shopping centre on my way to the Town Centre, where I could access internet services. All the shops at this shopping centre have closed; afraid of losing wares through vandalization by these militias. I pass with trepidation of what would become of those two weeks before 27 June 2008. Suddenly, the tranquillity of our ghetto has been shattered.

What we used to hear of happening all over the country becomes a sad reality. The township becomes so restless like a constipated fish. There is a day the president is addressing a rally in our local area, at Chibuku stadium. I know, on this day, the best thing one can do is just lock themselves inside the house. I do that, but I open up as my two sisters come over running for protection. There had gone to the shops to buy some foreign currency but chaos had erupted as the ZANUPF militias beat people up at the shops, and forcefully take them to the rally. There is total commotion as people flee all over the place. A lot people pass through our streets, running away from these marauding youths; now wearing all sorts of injuries on their bodies. There is no stability in the madness that ensures: We are simply crashed, shackled and maimed. It is a life and death struggle that assumes. The ZANUPF machinery chews us up and spit us without reason or warning.

*****

People who are still selling their wares in the streets have them confiscated willy-nilly. A Church Auntie has her Cousin who was teaching in Mutoko, in the rural areas, killed. She also tells me of a familiar story; that they approached this relative of hers at the school, asked for party cards, which she didn't have since she wasn't a member of any party. They raise her up and held her spread out, in mid-air, and they beat her on her buttocks and underneath the feet, until they had killed her. She was beaten to death for not belonging to any party. Her funeral had to be moved from Mutoko, her home area. They ended up having it in Chitungwiza, and bury her in the city. A local neighbour comes from his rural home in Rusape beaten to near death, and the story is the same. It seems we are not even goddamn mica anymore, but dust to the ZANUPF.

There is only pride in Mugabe during this time; in his campaigns trails, and pride works in a mysterious way. He just insults us in his pride; he even insults us in the above Chibuku stadium campaign rally. Saying he had never been to a city that smells as bad as Chitungwiza did. It doesn't matter to him that there are people who stay in this smelly place, that these people would have wanted to stay where he stays, where it is not smelly. There is only pride-now in him and no pride-later. It is hard for Mugabe to set aside pride-now for pride-later, and realise we are staying in this smelly place, just because of him. He stands in the middle of the whole country, as if he is the setting sun; the glare of this setting sun blinding everyone. We are lost even though we are living in our own country.

*****

Private and public transport is being forced to ferry people to ZANUPF rallies. If there is a rally, anywhere in the city, any form of transport, whether it is someone's personal car or public busses and taxis, is forced to divert route and transport ZANUPF supporters to these rallies. Transport owners would rather park their buses or cars on these rally days, but there are even forcefully told to pilot; or face the consequences. They are not paid, not even a single cent for these services. The militias tell them that it is now time to thank the president and, pay back for the good he did the entire country, all those years ago, when he liberated us from the colonial yoke. That we have been paying for this, and that we have paid more than enough, doesn't even cross these people's minds, so it's a lifetime servitude with us now. If you were so cheeky as to ask for payment, or push for payment, then pay you they will, with one hell of a walloping.

In Chitungwiza, every day, you hear of dead bodies being found, every morning. There is only killing by brutality, killing each other for the slice of belonging and administrative futility. The only news is of the kidnap, of children being dispossessed from mother's naps and of mortuaries that were said to be filled up with dead bodies. The dead people are no longer being sent to these mortuaries. A lot of people are missing, especially of the opposition party. Who will stay these butchering hands?

*****

Zimbabwe is militarised to the teeth. A day before the elections day; every corner of a small and big road in Harare has a policeman, and some soldiers manning it. The whole country is militarised with political or military or security bases. Violence and retribution is the

52

order of the day. It has taken the form of Somalia warlords' nature. There are places people are not allowed to go. When I went to the South African Embassy, to collect my passport which I had submitted for the Visa, all roads leading to this embassy were closed off to stem the tide of refugees who were seeking asylum at this embassy, in the Belgravia area of Harare. Some of the opposition MDC supporters have sought refugee status, so has the leader of the MDC. He has sought protection, at the Netherlands embassy, after withdrawing from the presidential race. It is so tense.

*****

On this day, I fail to collect my passport at the South African embassy. I return home to hear that every young person of our street, even at that, young teenagers; my young brother and his next door neighbour friend, have been taken to our local ward base. These teenagers were being referred to as comrades. Just think of this, some little boy who is barely 14 years old! They spend the night at the base, in June's cold winter nights. Some other days, the ZANUPF militias would come into our streets, by about midnight, for those who would have refused to join them. A week ago they managed to capture a couple of my street friends. They were taken to the base where they were beaten throughout the night until they collapsed. By the time I leave Zimbabwe for South Africa, that is, more than a week after their beatings; they are not yet able to sit on their buttocks, neither to stand, or even at that; to walk.

*****

The militia fills the air with wind tossed mantras about ZANUPF. They come for me a couple or so days after they took those street

53

friends. He is this local man who is sent to talk to me, Mr Chingwaru. He talks of the nationalistic pride of his party, the pride that is burning through his breasts. I reply him, unafraid of what he might really represent.

"The pride you are talking of is now foreign, from a distance of two generations of forgetting, Mr Chingwaru." He fixes me with a brownie eye and continues speaking simply because he has a speech wanting to come out of him. I let him do that, but I am not listening to his mumbling rhetoric. He is thinking that his speech is going to change me. I ask him

"Please, will you explain to me why you guys are forcing people, even young kids, to attend rallies and pungwes?"

"No, we are not forcing anyone to do that. People come out of their willingness, Mr Sharuko." He lies; and he denies it for his party.

"And, why are your kids not going there?"

"That's why I said we are not forcing people. People have to attend out of their own free will, so too are my daughters, Mr Sharuko.

I tell him they were creating concentration camps. He denies that.

"No, we are not creating concentration camps but national training camps and political bases. We had those during the liberation war, Mr Sharuko. They are important to the national and social fabric of a country." He says that filled with pride.

I tell him there is no war in the country and that these political bases and national training camps were based on the military, and that the military is a cluster fuck up, top to bottom like the ZANUPF itself.

"Mr Chingwaru, as you can see for yourself, the whole country is now clusters fuck up, as well."

I am impassioned as I tell him that the School of National Service where he was politically indoctrinated is a boring grey area where eggheads meet. That, you would never know there was anything happening out there. He waffles through some revolutionary catch prattle nonsense. He is piling up non-memory on memory over the years of indoctrination from the ZANUPF machinery. I tell him people won't eat this revolutionary élan, this mud-puddle. Our argument becomes so heated, boiling and then red-hot raw as reactionary comments, accusations and threats are heaved back and forth, like grenades. I know he wants the answer that I will be joining them, so I say to him.

"As much as I might want to join you, Mr Chingwaru, but it's now impossible, for I am leaving the morrow day for our rural home." He says,

"It's Ok, Mr Sharuko, you could join us later, perhaps when you return back from your rural home." And I instantly agree with him,

"Yes, I would do that, Mr Chingwaru", as he left me there dry, thirst and exhausted from this heated discussion.

*****

The morrow day I don't go outside. The next day I rise so early for the passport offices, and return when it was dark. I have failed to collect the passport, because of the noted issues above. There is the Friday of the Election Day, and the weekend. I am inside most of the times, other than the Election Day, when I go to vote. It's another thing, the voting; it's such a shame the way we are forced to elect our president. So, I never leave for my rural home, as such, but I am just locked inside. I am under a personally enforced house arrest, most of this time.

*****

In those days of cruelty peace was a precious commodity. I was stingy to give it away to the above fool. I couldn't give it to a people who didn't have it in their hearts, even when they were attempting to have it; even to those who had it without realising they had it.

There was no place to peacefully sit in Zimbabwe, so on the Monday after the elections; I go to the South African embassy, in the morning. They are now opened as they have cleared the MDC supporters. I don't know where those people had been dumped. I collect my passport, return home, and pack by bags and board the afternoon buses for South Africa. I simply have to leave for South Africa.

This Could Be Why Tsvangirai Had To Withdraw

In the first election in March 2008 he had defeated Mugabe by 47per cent against 43per cent so there had to be a run-of, since nobody had got the constitutionally 50 per cent plus one vote needed to form a government. These results were what we were told by ZEC (Zimbabwe Electoral Commission), an organisation that runs these elections in Zimbabwe, not that anyone else was able to prove them, or who got what percentage or what votes. Tsvangirai really had to withdraw from the June presidential runoff because of the following, among other reasons.

1. After the run-off date was announced, no advertising or campaign time was allowed to Tsvangirai on the public media, and the public media constitute over 80per cent total coverage of Zimbabwe.

2. Representatives of the MDC in ZEC were arrested and purged from this body.

3. The MDC was denied campaign rallies throughout the country by the police, Central Intelligence Organisation, the Army, and ZANUPF militias. Not once was Tsvangirai able to do a campaign rally. The only day he tried to organise his only campaign rally, in Harare at the Glamis stadium, the showground, on the eve of the election's week, it was disrupted by the military, police and Central Intelligence organisation (CIO). They were even pictured beating the few observers from the SADC. There were few observers, about 400, who were allowed to observe these elections in Zimbabwe, from outside of the country. They were only observers from countries that supported Mugabe and ZANUPF.

4. The ZANUPF militias, youths, soldiers, and CIO agents were killing grassroots MDC leaders and activists, for example; Tonderai Ndira of Mabvuku suburb. According to the MDC records, they were over 100 of its activist who were killed during this time. They are still some killings happening, even today (28 July 2008).

5. There was vote rigging whereby every military and security service person, it was said, had been forced to vote in the presence of their superiors. These service people could add up to nearly a million votes and through rigging, which was also alleged to be happening in some of our embassies and military barracks. When they were doing a recount of the 23 constituencies that the ZANUPF said they were irregularities, On 21 April 2008, a South African member of the Southern African Development Community (SADC) observer team, MP Dianne Kohler-Bernard, said that the recount was "fatally flawed". She reported of miscommunication of venue addresses, protocol registers at several counting stations, missing ballot box seals holding the keys for the two padlocks on each box broken. One set of ballot boxes was missing from a book of voting papers from the presidential election box, although all the other books were locked inside. Loose ballot box seals with serial numbers identical to those on already-sealed boxes were easily available.

6. There was total intimidation of the general populace. Nowhere would you go without hearing of stories of mass beatings and killings, forced participation in rallies and pungwes (all night vigils) at political bases. People from one ward were being forced to go to another ward where they would be forced to beat all the suspected opposition supporters. People from the Free Market, at Zengeza 2 shopping centre, were taken to beat Seke township people, in unit D by the

ZANUPF youth provincial leaders, accusing these Seke people to have voted for the MDC Member of Parliament, in the previous march election.

7. Most times the television, the radios and newspapers were critical and disparaging of the MDC, and were so full and foul of ZANUPF slogans, rallies, programs. On the public electronic media, in every 5 or so minutes there was a song; or a speech in praise of the ZANUPF. It was so painful to even try to listen, watch or read these public Medias.

8. The MDC couldn't field election agents throughout the country because just like in the previous 2000, 2002, 2005 elections, the whole country, especially the rural areas were closed off to the MDC, and nobody in his right sense could have volunteered for this dire job.

9. There were just a total of about 400 international observers to cover over 9000 voting stations and a country, the size of which, the United Kingdom constitute two thirds of; which meant they couldn't have done a better job of it. It's a great wonder that this time around the observers admitted that the elections were not free and fair, when in fact; they hadn't seen much of the election campaigns, against a 2000, 2002, and 2005 backdrop where they were a sizable number but shamelessly declared them as free and fair.

10. The people had been displaced at a scale never seen before in a country not at war. This was the heart of the ZANUPF's strategy. All busses and public transport were banned from operating on the Election Day such that it meant if you had run way from your ward, to avoid these killings, you couldn't return back on the Election Day to vote because the election was ward based.

11. All roads were manned by several militias and they refused people from going anywhere on Election Day.

This is the back drop in which the elections were done in Zimbabwe. Unfortunately, I can't account for everything that happened in this account. The election itself was the greatest of all the hoaxes I have ever seen. Sometimes I wonder why they had to go to such an extent, considering what they had already achieved before the elections.

27 June 2008

When I arrived at the voting station at Zengeza 7 primary school for the ward seven, where I was a registered voter; I was told I had to first go to a ZANUPF village headman. I was told this by a gang of ZANUPF youths stationed at the gates to the school. I asked them whether they were village headmen, in the towns. They told me they were there now. They told me that for me to be on the safe side, I had to go there. They told me that the ZANUPF militias, the headman, and the ZANUPF youths were going to do a reconciliation of all those who would have voted for the opposition party, against the details that they now had. They also threatened they would also carry out a reconciliation anyway, of all those who couldn't have voted. Everyone had to vote whether they liked it or not. They pointed for me where I had to go. It was at the home of the local ZANUPF headman, a certain Mr Jecha who stayed in Dovi Street. The place was just a couple of streets away from the voting station, in sight of the presiding officers of this polling station. Some of these officers were even stationed at the gates where these ZANUPF youths were turning people away from the station to this residence.

When I arrived at the residence there was this very long queue, of people registering their details. I followed the queue of those registering their details. When I got to the front of the queue he asked for my details, that is, my full name, address, telephone number and identity numbers. I gave him all these, and then this village headman gave me a blank piece of paper, which I was told; I had to fill it in with the serial number of my ballot's paper.

At the voting station I voted, but also wrote down my serial number, on that blank piece of paper, when I was behind the booth. I took that piece of paper to the village headman who recorded that serial number against my details. It meant that whether I liked it or not I had to vote for Mugabe. It was in the afternoon, at about 3, when the headman and the militias were arrested. Most of the people had been forced to participate in this shame election. To think that it was happening in many parts of Harare, also that most of the presiding officers knew about it, especially those in my ward where the voting station was a stone's throw away, in sight of this headman's residencies, left a lot to be desired.

But this is how we elected our president, who is the president of Zimbabwe, on 27 June 2008

Coconut Republic

*C**OCONUT .n. 1 The large brown seed of a tropical palm, consisting of a woody husk lined with edible white flesh and containing a clear liquid. 2, the white flesh of a coconut- origin Spanish and Portuguese Coco-"grinning face"...* Paperback Oxford English Dictionary.

REPUBLIC .n. A state in which power is held by the people and their elected representatives, and which has a president rather than a King or Queen... Paperback Oxford English Dictionary.

If we combine the two meanings, literarily speaking, a coconut republic can be summed up as a, "grinning face" republic. Who is grinning at this republic is my question?

According to George B. Ayittey (Professor at American University in Washington DC) in his The Sunday Times article on Zimbabwe of 31 August 2008, a Coconut Republic is a nation; where nothing no longer makes sense, where common sense has been done away with and arrogant insanity rampages with impunity. Ayittey feels, rightly so, that Zimbabwe is a despicable disgrace to the entire continent and joins the long list of African countries that we Africans, especially black Africans, have mismanaged to the ground. There is a long list of this gruesome post-colonial African countries road to implosion.

Liberia(1990), Mali(1991), Somalia(1993), Central African Republic(1993), Rwanda(1994), Burundi(1995), Zaire(1996), Sierra Leone(1999), Ivory Coast(2000), Togo(2005). The following leaders have been at the helm, of destruction of their countries; Mobuto Sese

Seko, Laurent Kabila, Samuel Doe, Charles Taylor, Kenneth Kaunda, Moussa Traore, Andre Koligba, Said Barre, and the list is endless as one leader after another continued destroying these countries. Countries like the DRC (Zaire), Madagascar, and Guinea Bissau have been dealing with political strife in almost their entire histories. The most important problem has been the stubborn refusal of the leadership to relinquish or share power when their people are fed up with them. African countries laughed off the June 27 2008 "coconut" runoff, which Mugabe, the sole candidate, won a landslide victory. For an idea of the kind of election, and electioning processes, that I personally witnessed, there are particular pieces like TWO WEEKS BEFORE 27 JUNE 2008, and 27 JUNE 2008 you could check on in this book. You can only laugh, grin, or cringe with shame at this election.

I agree with Ayittey that the traditional (indigenous) African system was confederacy, such that they was participatory democracy based upon consensus-building under its chiefs, like Songhai, Ghana, Mali, and the Great Zimbabwe. I also feel that even though there was participatory democracy, the problem was still on who would be appointed, as the chief or the king. Chiefs or Kings were appointed from Semi-monarchy families. Like European monarchies, they could only be replaced when they were dead, or were incapable due to an illness. The belief that the chiefs were infallible, and could not be brought before justice to answer for any crime they could have committed was another problem. These traits are still prevalent in many African societies, especially in our leaders.

I remember the song from Zimbabwean singer, Clive Malunga, entitled Zunde RaMambo (the King's Crop Bank). Kings in Zimbabwe used to receive, from their subjects, all sorts of harvests from the fields, as well as domestic beasts, for keeping. This stored-up crop bank was used to feed their subjects in the times of hunger, draughts and was sometimes used by the King to pay for fines brought upon him. In this song Clive was saying the king's crop bank was depleted, so what would the king pay him with, for the wrong he has done to him? The chorus offers him answers to this dilemma.

"In our land the King can't be prosecuted."

"In our land the King can't be fined."

"In our land nobody disputes the King's ruling".

The Zimbabweans thought that he was singing about Mugabe when the song was released, but he denied that. He said it was just a traditional Zimbabwean song, and that it had nothing to do with Mugabe. But still, the lyrics bring into clarity our thinking on the Chieftainship, and or Kingship. This is still the thinking of our leaders, as well; that they are above the law. Whatever they say, or do passes. For Ayittey to totally assign this trait to foreign influences like "One party state" or "President for life", or an economic system of dirigisme (state interventionism) is not entirely true. I think both our traditional systems and these adopted systems have been used by our leaders to stay in power. In so doing, they have created vampire states that suck the economic vitality out of the people, and metastasize into coconut republics and implode.

Ayittey rightly goes further in saying the implosion nearly always begins with a disputed electoral process, a refusal to hold elections or outrageously rigged polls. According to Ayittey, Zimbabwe's final chapter has been written by the creation of a "hostage president", whereby the joint operations command is subtly in charge. Ominously, the junta is led by the military who subtly took over the country, just after the March elections. Generals Chiwenga, Shiri, Sibanda and minister Mnangagwa are the real power brokers in Zimbabwe. These, like the other rebels, who have staged coups in Africa before them, Laurent Kabila, Charles Taylor etc…, are just "crocodile liberators", and are not any better.

The Blame Game

This essay deals with historical issues and I suppose I can be allowed to be a hanging judge, not with the noose but with a pen. In this essay I am going to re-assign the blame back to where it belongs. Historically, the white Zimbabweans have to blame; especially the colonialist for colonial Zimbabwe was such that the majority blacks and other minor races were disadvantaged on the economic pie. They were denied a good education, even when they could afford it, social services…, and even a belief in themselves, in their abilities and identities. All these disadvantages can still be seen, even today, in Zimbabwe. When the black government inherited this flawed society they haven't done much to make that difference. Now, it's inexcusable for the likes of Mugabe to continue going back to colonialism for all the ills of Zimbabwe.

I can't deny that something significant has been done by Mugabe on education, or on just developing of people's awareness, of their abilities, but that's all that has been done. When it comes to all the other things that makes a lot of difference, like skills development, economic empowerment, labour laws, entrepreneurship development, company development, fiscal issues like interest rates and monetary issues like credit facilities for car, property and house purchasing, and or ownership; there is still a world to be accomplished in these. It's totally impossible to be able to buy a car using your workplace's pay in Zimbabwe, unless if you are a director of a company; not even senior managers can be able to do that. It seems people with political connections are the only ones who can be able to do that.

When Mugabe grabbed farms in Zimbabwe, rather than settling qualified black farmers, or disadvantaged people in these farms, he parcelled them out to his cronies, who over the years, had already had some farms of their own. I remember reading articles in the newspapers, of the Land reform commission that Mugabe commissioned just after conclusion of the land reform programme. The article posited that a ZANUPF central committee and politburo member had grabbed up to 7 farms; and that the majority of ZANUPF bigwigs had at least multiple-ownership. This has also been the kind of trend in all the spheres of the economy. So, to keep blaming colonialism is now a hard pill for a lot of Zimbabweans to swallow because we know that these problems we have are because of the mismanagement of the economy and corruption, not entirely of colonialism.

Zimbabwe now defies every logic when it comes to corruption and the mismanagement of an economy. You can only get a thing in Zimbabwe after bribing a chain long supply chain. Mugabe knows the whole country blames him so he devises this culture, not only him, but maybe the biggest part of African leadership, of defraying the blame from him.

They usually do that by using catch prattle programmes like African nationalism, African renaissance, African revolutionary..., and etcetera other many programmes. So that, they would speak glibly of being African in these Africanisation and African pride programmes, yet its meaning even eludes them, all the time. Africa combines a multiplicity of people, cultures, voices, regional, cultural, linguistic. Political and historical lines as well. To be African precludes skin colour, origin, culture, beliefs etc...This African nationalism they preach of doesn't help us in the real quest for a real African spiritual character.

Dr Anthony Holiday, the University of Western Cape philosopher says, "Africa's search for houses of the intellect, shaped by African identities, is in the last resort, a spiritual search, an attritional war of ethical resistance, waged in the name of treasures which are spiritual, with a spiritual homecoming as it's hoped for victory." I even feel the general populace, in the streets in Africa, particularly in Zimbabwe, are past this resounding phrases idealistic African rhetorical stage. People in the streets of Zimbabwe now care about freedom, economic emancipation, and bread and butter issues. Everyone wants to know that they can be able to put food on their tables for themselves and their families, that their families have a safe and good future, and that they are free to be whoever they want to be. But what Holiday is saying is that; as a people, we should simply interrogate these Africanness programs like African renaissance, NEPAD, and the other many programs, in our search for a real spiritual character of Africanness.

Sometimes you read in the newspapers of an apologist whining that what's this hullabaloo about Mugabe is all about. They will be inferring that there are bigger fish to fry in Africa like maybe the Kibakis, Gaddafis, and Al Bashirs of Africa, who are always let alone by the whole world, so why Mugabe? That's their question. Maybe their augment is, in their minds Mugabe has killed a few people as compared to the above, and that he should be left alone to kill an entire race or until he has created another holocaust like Hitler's or that of the Great lakes of bloodbath for anyone, or for any African country or person to criticise him.

"Mugabe has always held elections after every 5 years, Mugabe is a democrat, and Mugabe is a true African son..." Well, after all he is fighting our colonialist, and all this is good measure for these apologists to ask the whites, especially Britain, to leave Mugabe alone. What elections and I suppose it's the 27 June 2008 elections? We, as Zimbabweans, also believe that if someone does wrong, he has done wrong and definitely he has to be criticised, not necessarily by Africans alone. Africanness, one should know, is the language of the soul. It doesn't matter where you originated from, where the criticism originates from. It might be from Europe, Asia, and Americas. What matters is the truth it sheds out. We can be loyal to our countries but not loyal to the governments, the same applies to Africa. We can be loyal to Africa without being loyal to those nationalistic catch prattle Africanisation programmes.

This could be the reason why, after all these Mbeki's years of African issues being dealt with by African people ideologies, people in Zimbabwe haven't jelled to this idea. After all we are in a global village! This time warp, which our leaders have on these issues, has resulted in many African professionals leaving the continent for more secure countries.

The government we have in Zimbabwe is not a government that inspires confidence, trust and respect. There is always an undemocratic streak, even in the moderate ones in this government. As long as their jobs are not up for grabs they would appear as if they are good leaders, like what Mugabe was before the Zimbabweans decided they couldn't afford him anymore in the 2000 elections.

Mbeki wanted to stay in power, so was Chiluba, when the bell tolled for them. Maybe it's a streak inherited from colonialism, like what

Smith and the apartheid leaders did when the bell tolled out for them. Maybe it is inherent in our psyche as African people. Some of these black leaders still carry unhealed wounds from this colonial period; Mugabe who had to forgo burying his son because the Smith regime had refused him release from jail to go and burry his only son. But for them to turn against their people, for them to think that the world or their people owe them some space to totally misbehave, for them to believe that they have to rule their countries, and according to the late Vice president of Zimbabwe, Simon Muzenda, "until the horses have grown horns", is to take naiveté too far and to hold onto issues now irrelevant, too far from their time.

I suppose Gwede Mantashe (ANC secretary general) likes this idea, of the ANC also ruling South Africa until the horses have grown horns. Until, maybe according to Gwede Mantashe, South African horses have beaten Zimbabwean horses at this game of growing horns. Talking of horses growing horns, one can't even help drawing some parallelism. One can't help wondering what the ANC and South Africa will do with Zuma's horns, for there is no doubt that a time shall come when Zuma would use his horns in order to survive, in his political life and corruption charges, or his incapability as a good leader.

It was just a parallel, and still on parallels, I want to look at Mugabe and Mandela. Mandela was imprisoned for 27 years, Mugabe for 11 years. I know I don't know how bad the treatment either way was, but after taking over as the president, Mandela never took the country to hostage using his 27 years in jail as moral justifications to misbehave badly towards his captors and his people. Mugabe likes to go back to the past as a reason for all the ills of Zimbabwe, not to him. I think if he can have a chance to lambaste himself, if it could

71

give him headway in the long run, he could do that. I want to think this warp is used by Mugabe as his thumb tank. He would hide behind it whenever he comes under scrutiny. The truth is colonialism or not, he is just a dictator, but a cleaver one at that; who knows how to use emotions to deceive his critics.

Mandela is now retiring, so is Desmond Tutu in South Africa, Masire in Botswana has retired, so has Chisano and Nyerere. Kwame Nkurume and Levy Mwanawasa are dead. These leaders used to inspire a lot of confidence, in the masses, with their beliefs and leadership styles. For some time Mugabe was in this clan before he totally lost it. Now he belongs in the same tier of African leaders below the likes of Mbekis who view their citizens, even the whole world as unthinking, and are also viewed by their citizens with utter contempt. It means Mugabe now belongs to the worlds of the Bokassas, Amin, Mobuto, and Mengestu (whom some even say is Mugabe's special advisor) of Africa.

I remember, during the 2008 elections, nobody in his right sense would have volunteer to even switch the television on in case they would come across Mugabe spouting his venom at everyone else, but himself. These African leaders would rather the whole world leave them alone, in their jobs, than let their own people decide that through the ballot. I get this feeling that they are being allowed that by the whole world. Rwanda, Uganda, Sudan, Kenya, Libya, and Zimbabwe are just a few examples the whole world should answer for. Whilst we are still at it, Kenya just like Zimbabwe, is a window into the kind of African democracy the entire African continent are in the process of perfecting, and are now selling to the entire world, whereby the incumbents, even when they had lost an election, they would be helped to stick to their seats by the AU, by devising these national unity governments. Mugabe and the ZANUPF calls it their right, that they can't let the country they fought for with a sword be given away through a pen (the elections).

I also have a very big bone to chew with the purported world's superpowers like the mighty G8 countries, the EU countries, and China. It seems these countries like to play some sick insane games, at the detriment of some nations, especially the poor African countries. I have seen them, over the years, dithering when it comes to small African countries, like what happened in Rwanda, Uganda, Burundi, DRC and Zimbabwe lately. When it comes to decision making in times of crises, or even purported crisis, in countries like Iraq, Korea and Israel, even in the Chinese-Tibetan issue, and lately in Georgia, they raise hell and instantly deal with whatever situation is obtaining, even in a high-handed manner. You end up feeling that behind every conflict in the world these days, the USA, the UK, and the western world countries would take one side whilst China, Russia and most of the developing world would take another side. This polarising of issues is not exactly due to different, deeply held beliefs between the two sides but because they will be testing each other's powers, as if the cold war is still very much on the roll, and protecting their vested interests. Look at the Zimbabwean issue. It is now 8 years or so old but they are still dithering, some even going to the extent of protecting Mugabe from any censure. Only to hear them, at their full voices, preaching about protecting the rights of their favoured nation's citizens. You would wonder are there African human rights where the abusers are left alone and western or Chinese human rights where everyone raises the hackles.

This molly-coddling of Mugabe by the world leaders and by Mbeki especially, has resulted in Mbeki failing to push Mugabe to negotiate and behave in good faith over the years. Even as I write this essay, at least 6 years since Mbeki started dibbling in the Zimbabwean issue, there is nothing much to write home about, about his silent diplomacy methodology, to solve the Zimbabwean issue. It is a completely silent methodology. I suppose, even if he were to ever managing to sort this issue, it would be a case of "too little too late". The damage has already been done and Mbeki is as worse a culprit as Mugabe himself. One can't help suggesting that if ever there is punishment to be met on Mugabe, in the future; Mbeki should be part of the deal. It took Venter (former South African apartheid leader) a couple of weeks of sanctions to bring Smith to the negotiating table. For Mbeki it is why be bothered with the sanctions and their far-reaching consequences. After all, Mugabe is his best buddy.

One would also be forgiven for thinking that Mbeki had an ulterior motive for dragging this situation, like for instance an augment proffered that South Africa has gained immensely in taping skills shortage from Zimbabwe's resulting emigration of skilled people. In so doing, filling up posts left by the whites leaving South Africa for greener pasture, and also filling in on Zimbabwe's competitive niches in the region and abroad, in trade. Historically, South Africa has always wanted a weaker Zimbabwe to compete with in the region, or even in Africa itself. A kind of Zimbabwe that defied South Africa in 1997 and occupied the DRC is not the kind of Zimbabwe South Africa would ever wish for across the Limpopo River.

Mbeki's speeches like "Leave Zimbabwe for me" to Bush when Bush tried to interfere in Zimbabwe. Even his cold shoulder rejection of any other suggested diplomatic envoys, like Koffi Annan and Olusegun Obasanjo, galvanises this believe and points to his obsessive want to control the kind of outcome he wanted for Zimbabwe. So, if Zimbabwe is his sole call, then Mbeki and South Africa has to accept blame on Zimbabwe's demise.

Whilst I am still at it, I have a big problem with African fathers (former African statesmen) who are looking on and turning a blind eye on fellow statesmen bungling and misruling the countries of a continent they fought for. Africa has a sizable number of these former (good) statesmen, but all the criticisms; or just the interest, in this rape of these citizens, by these despotic leaders, have been just a few muffled protests. Maybe they have really retired and are now wallowing in their greatness and holiness, to waste time on small things like Zimbabwe. After all, the more these new statesmen messes at a bigger scale, the more these former statesmen approach almost sainthood status in the eyes of the entire world!

But, why won't the AU and SADC refuse to recognise Mugabe?

Why did they ask for a government of national unity in Zimbabwe, when they knew the elections had not been free and fair?

What precedent were they setting? What kind of a unity government, and how about the wishes of the electorate in Zimbabwe.

Why the AU does scorns any international interference in Zimbabwe, especially if it is coming from the western world?

Why does the AU allow these leaders to disregard the wishes of their people?

I think these are some of the questions that would always downplay whatever achievements and good intentions the AU has.

The Zimbabwean people are somewhat to blame, as well. It's either they are downright stupid or they really do believe in whatever beliefs they have. You wonder that after all this damage Mugabe has done to the country, and to their lives, you could still get 43per cent still wanting to keep Mugabe, in the recognised March 2008 elections. It boggles the mind what really do these people want Mugabe to give them, that he failed to give them in the last 28 years. The galling thing is that this 43per cent also buys from the same shops that everyone else buys from, were affected by Mugabe's polices over the years, like Operation Murambatsvina, and suffers from the same economic woes that everyone else suffers from. Some are even starving from hunger; some even borrow from and are looked after by the other 47 per cent who voted against Mugabe. Yet, you will see them voting, election after election for Mugabe, fighting all the way to keeping Mugabe in power, the source of their woes.

Drawing some parallel with the 47per cent who voted for Tsvangirai, you can't help but ask why the bloody well people don't just get into the streets unorganised and push for Mugabe's ouster. There are many reasons that have been proffered. Some people believe that they would be thugged out of the streets by Mugabe's thugs of the police, army and CIO. Some people saying it would destroy the economy all the more; but what economy is there? Some people also say it's ineffective against Mugabe. I can't really be able to deny them any of the above alibis, but one can't also help asking at what point one draws a line between bravery and cowardice. But, of course, they would have the last word because this 47per cent expressed their views at the ballots.

My body boils when I hear, lately, of talk of wanting to make it mandatory for every young person to undergo some form of training (national service training) in South Africa. A look across the border; Zimbabwe did the same thing with the Border Gezi training and national service training. A look at how the Zimbabweans came to pay because of this oversight should be a pointer to the South Africans. The trainees became the feared ZANUPF militias who terrorised the Zimbabwean electorate. To the ANC, this would present a future tramp card; they would use them to beat the electorate into liking the ANC, and voting for the ANC.

Our biggest let-down as a continent has always been our hero-worshiping of our leaders because they liberated us from the shackles of colonialism. In so doing, we give our leaders a lot of leeway. By the time we wake up they would have done great damage to our countries and our economies. This hero worshiping of Mugabe and his ZANUPF cronies was perfected well in Zimbabwe, to the extent of messing and destroying the media, courts, and the constitution, just in order to protect Mugabe from any prosecution, or from criticisms, even mild criticisms. The Zimbabweans went to the extent of making it a criminal offence for anyone to say anything bad, even jokes against Mugabe. Our king cannot be scolded in Zimbabwe.

Now, the Zimbabweans have learned it the harder way, that is, no one is above the country's laws. That democracy gives everyone the right to be his or her own oppressor.

The Point Of Contention: The Police

I want to write about Jestina Mukoko for I had known her years back and, liked her reading news on the national television and radio. It was days when ZBC was a little bit professional, when there was no need to access satellite broadcasting by Zimbabweans. It was the days of Obert Mandimutsira, Musi Khumalo, Eric knight, Peter Johns, James Maridhadhi, Tonderai Ndoro. It was years when we came-off age and became adults, the 1980s and 1990s. Those were some of the presenters and DJ s who helped us through this journey to maturity. Nostalgia aside, let me get into the details of Jestina Mukoko, but you know; I can't just help saying "Good evening, news at 8 read to you by Jestina Mukoko."

Later on, after Jonathan Moyo had messed up the ZBC, all those professionals left ZBC, some out of the country like Erick knight, Brenda Moyo, Carol Gombakomba, and others for the private sector like Jestina Mukoko, who is the director at Zimbabwe Peace Project. Her job was to collect information on political violence, especially names of perpetrators and their victims, and to help the victims deal with the abuse. After collecting it, it is alleged, by the ZANUPF or government, that she was sending it to British institutions and broadcasting it on the internet. Jestina, with more than 30 other Zimbabwe Peace Project staff and MDC activists and staffers were abducted in November 2008 by the CIO. They were kept at a secret location, and I should think, maybe at the C.I.O's notorious torture chambers in Goromonzi. I can't quality this assertion though, but whilst I am still at that, I remember a story. I was told this story by my brother's in-laws.

He was abducted from Budiriro where he was MDC activist for the area, sometime during the 2002 general election. He was brought to this farm in Goromonzi by night. They took him to a pool, which was filled up with sulphuric acid. They told him names of people who had been thrown into this pool and had melted inside this pool. He was told never to get involved in the MDC activities, if he didn't want to end up like those people who had been thrown into this pool. That In-law had stopped involving himself in political activism for the MDC, ever after that, and left the country for South Africa. They are quite a lot other stories that have been told, about this farm and the torture chambers.

In this group of Jestina there was a little boy, who had been abducted together with his parents, and his name is Nigel, and her parents' names are Colin and Violet. When it happened, I wrote a poem about him "For Nigel", dedicated to this little prisoner of war that was first published in Italy by *Pomezia Notizia Magazine* in March 2009, also published in my collection *Mad Bob Republic*. I have reproduced it below.

"In the carnival of a conspiracy
Words distorting truth to lies.
Writer in a block falls down
With unexpressed anger.

But a toddler bubbles in-

79

Sad iambic pentametric tears.
In a biographical poem like–
Free falling operatic comedies.
That does not keep their laughter.

Nigel, you spent 72 days,
Locked with your parents
Colin and Violet, for sins unknown,
In Chikurubi maximum prison.

But only gamblers–
Have rushed to your bubble wails.
Searching for some currents,
An ode, a ditty, or a sonnet.
But diving for gold, and leaving you.
Letting you endure your losses alone."

That child had to spend a collective 72 days as a prisoner! Back to Mukoko's story, she was later locked in Chikurubi Maximum security prison in leg-irons, without proper medical care for the injuries she had sustained when tortured by the security operatives. She was found by her lawyers on 23 December, and on the next day, the nine of them were brought before the magistrates' courts. On the same evening she was granted a High court order for release to the Avenues clinic for medical examinations and treatment under police guard, as well as the release of 23 others without bail, whom also included Nigel. The police out rightly refused to execute this order. Instead they were re-locked in Chikurubi maximum prison. These are some lines I wrote about the police's brutalities and behaviour in a poem entitled, "Brutal Times", published in April 2009 by *Yellow*

Medicine Review (USA), also published in my collection *Mad Bob Republic*.

"My lawyer asked for bail and for
A doctor to look at my wounds.
Which I was granted by the court, but which
The police defied the court over
And re-locked me back in my cell as
They appeal, re-appeal, and re- appeal the appealed
Judgments, whilst
The beatings continue.
Now timed like eating times, three times
A day like breakfast, lunch and supper."

When she was later examined, strong evidence of torture was found. On 31 December 2008, the lawyers lodged an urgent high court application on behalf of Mukoko, for an order compelling the police to disclose the identities of those responsible for her abduction and detention. Didymus Mutasa, then the Minister of Security filled an affidavit confirming state security (the fearsome CIO) involvement for her seizure and detention, but also claimed that divulging the information sought would jeopardise national security. He said, rather, that Jestina was being held for organising, and recruiting bandits that were alleged to have been undergoing training in Botswana. Mugabe could even go to the extent of accusing Ian Khama (Botswana president) of doing this, though the SADC later disputed this claim.

Another story of Goromonzi torture chambers, also related to the above charge, was the one I read in The Zimbabwean Newspaper, of a certain MDC activist who had been abducted in relation to this tramped up charge of banditry. He was brought to these Goromonzi chambers and was tortured for days. Finally he was blackmailed into believing that if he admitted to his involvement in this Botswana banditry charge, he would be released and would not be charged with the murder of a soldier, whom these torturers had killed. This soldier was one of those soldiers who had been caught during the Soldiers strikes earlier on; when the soldiers had demonstrated against pay issues and the country's conditions. Now, this man was even being falsely accused of having killed this soldier. In order for him to be released, he had to read a statement written by his torturers to the ZBC crew. That the national broadcaster could get involved, at this level, is disgusting, to say the least. He read it, admitting to his involvement in the banditry charge, also saying that he had been trained in Botswana, yet he had never been to Botswana his entire life.

About mid-January Jestina's lawyers managed to have her case referred to the Supreme Court, which I must admit was a great feat for them to get to the Supreme Court in just three months. I am saying this because the MDC and Morgan Tsvangirai failed in 6 years, that is from the 2002 elections up to the 2008 elections, to have their court appeal on vote rigging against Mugabe be heard at any court in Zimbabwe, not even the High court, to start with. This time the Supreme Court couldn't find a technicality to hide behind in refusing Jestina her constitutional right to see a doctor. After seeing the doctor's affidavit stressing the inadequacy of the prison hospital and the necessity of getting Mukoko medical attention in a hospital with proper facilities, he directed that she should receive "appropriate medical attention as a matter of urgency". How appropriate, was to the determination of the police, and when, was still to the police's discretion.

After a week she was later taken, in leg-irons and under armed escort to the Avenues clinic in the Harare's avenues area. She was examined by the doctors, still in leg-irons, sent for an x-rays, still in leg-irons, an ultrasound scan to assess for injuries. Still in leg irons, she was admitted for treatment and was put on a drip. But as to "how appropriate", the prison warders refused to allow her to remain in hospital. Against her will, still in leg irons, and on the drip; they took her back to Chikurubi. The Avenues clinic refused to sign her discharge papers as she was removed against their professional medical advice.

When negotiations for the power sharing deal were on-going we used to argue with my brother who wasn't privy to Mugabe's autocratic tendencies and oppressive machinations. When the negotiations reached a stale-mate on the Police or Home Affairs ministry, and the importance of this ministry in the negotiations; that's when we did argued a lot about it all. My brother left Zimbabwe for South Africa in 1996, and all that he had read in the newspapers in South Africa hadn't really convinced him of Mugabe's madness, and the MDC's genuineness. So, we would argue about this ministry and the negotiations until I was so angry, to the extent of wanting to fight it out physically. We never really did that. In the first days his wife used to participate, but later on had had enough of our arguments and whenever we started she would sneak off to bed.

When Jestina was arrested, my brother was so convinced that Botswana and the MDC were exactly involved in this cooked up banditry charge and theory. To show him what ZANUPF and

Mugabe were capable of, in framing their competitors, I ended up telling him of the arrest and the trial of Morgan Tsvangirai, for allegedly strategizing to assassinate Mugabe, and that of Reverend Ndabaningi Sithole, the silencing of Reverend Canaan Banana, Archbishop Pius Ncube, the death of Learnmore Jongwe, the never explained killings of Movern Mahachi, Border Gezi... etc, and the many generals.

I especially talked to him about Tsvangirai's ordeal, the cooked-up charges, the cooked up tapes evidence. I told him that no one could hear well what was being discussed on those tapes, and of that disgusting trickster, Canadian witness Ari Ben Menashe, and of Montreal where the meetings to strategize on the killing of Mugabe, between Menashe and Tsvangirai, were said to have happened. I told him of the hullabaloo that the public media, especially the ZBC, made out of this trail. That eventually the judge, Judge Paddington Garwe, threw away the case and found no evidence incriminating Tsvangirai.

Slowly, my brother began to understand the reason why those three security ministries had to be shared to achieve balance between the negotiating parties. That is, the Home Affairs ministry (police), the Defence ministry (army), and the Security ministry (C.I.O). Why the MDC was so set on having at least the Home Affairs ministry to balance the other two security ministry that ZANUPF had awarded itself, as a prerequisite in the negotiations. It is the police who have the mandate to protect people, properties, and enforce the laws. As you can see from Jestina's case, it is exactly the police who were refusing to enforce the laws, torturing people and refusing to protect them in collusive with the C.I.O, and sometimes the army.

It was for that sole reason that I hold Kgalema Motlanthe and other SADC heads of state as wimps, and thinking of the SADC, AU, UN, and especially of South Africa's leaders, Motlanthe and Mbeki, sucks. It makes me feel so sick. How on God's earth did they fail to wrestle the police ministry from Mugabe's control? Tsvangirai was made to settle for the co-chairing of this ministry by these SADC wimps, even though ZANUPF had already amassed a lot of powerful ministries (like the defence, security, justice, agriculture, mining, and information publicity ministries).

Max Du Preez couldn't help asking the same question (The Star, 29 January 2009). "How would Motlanthe, who acts in your, and in my name (South African name, or Africa's name), explain to Jestina Mukoko, a proud and dignified Zimbabwean patriot, why he is helping to shield the man responsible for her torment...? This is the regime that Motlanthe and his SADC brothers are propping up. A president and a party who had lost the elections they themselves had overseen and organised. A president and a party under whose leadership over 4 000 people have died of a preventable disease, cholera (the fortune Mad Grace spent shopping in the Far East recently alone could have saved dozens of lives)."

Max Du Preez continues; if you were Tsvangirai, this is the message from SADC, "accept the power sharing deal, sharing the control of the police, or else you can go hang." If he had refused that, these SADC wimps would have given Mugabe the go-ahead to form his own government, and to simply continue the raping and pillaging of Zimbabwe. These are the African solutions for African problems, of Mbeki's rather narcissistic African renaissance. "We don't like you Tsvangirai", the African leaders have said, in fact they want Mugabe, ZANUPF, the Army, CIO, and police to remain as they have been,

85

and to continue to marginalise and frustrate Tsvangirai and his party, whilst they claim legitimacy for anything good that comes from this new government. So, it seems, it's another case closed, guilty dispatched for now, and judgement reserved for these SADC wimps, again.

World's "Best" Central Banker

Eventually, when Gideon Gono, the Reserve Bank governor was beaten all systems out by the Zimbabwean dollar's fickleness he recommended that the Rand be informally adopted alongside the Zimbabwean dollar. But he said that he never wrote the 105 page document that had these recommendations; that experts are saying it has Gono's trademark. These experts are saying its Gono who wrote that document because it has Gono's hallmark, that is, shallow analysis. The Star, of 22 January 2009, says; it's not uncommon for developing and transitional economies to formally or informally adopt a second currency. The USA did it during its great depression years, by form of battering certificates; Argentina did it in the 2002 crippling recession by adopting the USA dollar; El Salvador in 2001, and many South American economies uses the dollar informally nowadays; Ukraine and Kazakhstan in the 1990's allowed the dollar to circulate .

As I write this piece, the exchange rate is Z$100 trillion equivalent to US$30, No! In actual fact, it is, Z$1000 000 000 000 000 000 000 000 000 000 000 000-00, if I have to add back the 3 plus 10 plus 12 zeroes that had been removed before by Gono. This is unfathomable against a 1980 backdrop in which Z$1 was worth US$1.50. Harare economist John Robertson and a lot others, like the Cato institute, believe the inflation is in sextillions of percentages, not the suggested November rate of 80 billion percentage. They believe it's the world's highest ever, beating Hungary's highest ever of 13 quadrillion percentage in 1946. The main cause of this has been hyperinflation in which prices doubled in a matter of hours, and cash in one's hands devalue before the opportunity to spend it presents itself.

As a side story to this piece; it makes me recall how my brother who had spent about 12 years out of the country, in South Africa, without returning back to Zimbabwe had to grapple, really that badly, with the economics of Zimbabwe when we returned home together in May 2008. At Beitbridge border town we exchanged 100 Rands for 2 billion Zimbabwean dollars. He was so excited and happy for the figure, and could joke with his little boy-son about the fact that going home to Zimbabwe had made him into a billionaire. That, he had touched his first billion, that even his son whom he had also given this bundle of bearer cheques to touch, had also touched a billion dollars, at that young age (2 years). People in that bus laughed at this joke; though to my brother it was not really a joke, as such. He was very keen on this idea, of having had his first billion.

By the time we reached Masvingo town, all the money we had had been used up, just to buy a meal for the four of us, that is my brother, his wife, the kid, and me. When we arrived in Harare, about 300km from Masvingo, we had to exchange another 100 Rands, and now it was for Z\$3.2 billions for transport to Chitungwiza, which is 25 kilometres from Harare. When we arrived in Chitungwiza, that same day, at night, it was nowZ\$4 billion dollars for the same 100 Rands. This day alone inducted my brother into Zimbabwe's mind boggling economics. He was, for the rest of the stay there, very quiet, disturbed, foreboding and anxious to leave for South Africa, and totally astounded.

Back to those gonoisms, the Gono in these gonoisms feels it is imperative due to the economic relationship between South Africa and Zimbabwe for Zimbabwe to adopt the Rand to anchor the Zimbabwean dollar. Tendai Biti, the secretary general of the opposition, MDC party, feels this is the thinking of Gono and his inner circle. Robertson points out that the economy had already been randified. The difference, for some years, had been the circulation route, where it has been from illegal to legal. John Hopkins University at Baltimore applied economist, Steve Hanke, in his book, "Zimbabwe-from hyperinflation to growth", also agrees to some extent, and adds. "If viewed in a narrow profit-and-loss point of view, it is extremely profitable for South Africa, that is, through seigniorage; the revenue a central bank earns from issuing a currency whose face value exceeds the cost of printing or minting each unit of it." Victor Munyama, an economist at Standard bank also feels it would facilitate trade between the two countries, but there are a couple of catches to these gonoisms.

These gonoisms presupposes a world in which Zimbabwe would return to its healthy manufacturing levels of 1990's, and that Zimbabwe should also have a workable political settlement, because if more Rands are set to chase somewhat scarce goods, it would have an adverse effect on South Africa's inflation rates. This will put pressure on South Africa to adjust its manufacturing levels accordingly.

Gono rejects that all these gonoisms were his inventions, but that's besides the import of this article, whether it is Gono or not who wrote that 105 pager, but the idea is that they are his trademarks. I would like to hear his defence against these allegations. He posits that he would never, in his lifetime, like Smith and Mugabe before him, on the use of this phrase, "Never in my lifetime", recommend for the adoption of the Rand or any other currency. I will give him the benefit of doubt at this time in this article, but let's explore some more of those gonoisms in the report.

"The Zimbabwean government requires about 3.5 billion Rands a month to pay public salaries, honour the imported fuel bill, keep the health system in working order (that is if there is any health to still talk of in Zimbabwe), and buy the required fertilizers and seed to pump into the critical agricultural sector, with a third of this overall expenditure allocated for other government uses, a code for either a slush fund or the defence bill." If one has been following Gono, over the years, one would definitely know that all these budgets have been his inventions and have been directly under his control over the years. Ever since he introduced them, and in doing so, he disagreed with his boss over them, Herbert Murerwa (then finance minister). He won the battle through the ouster of Murerwa from the ministry of finance by our clueless president.

Other unintelligible gonoisms in this report that shout out from this report, are about our export duties (from what exports), and the country's rich resources of gold, diamond, platinum, iron ore and chrome (which I would like to think are buried kilometres down into the soil) as key sources of revenue, that according to Gono, would pay for monthly expenditures. Like the belief we have to sell the land with these purported minerals to our Chinese friends, and then get some monthly subscriptions from our Chinese dears. Here are the figures to our Chinese friends. We have 3 billion tons of platinum in the Great dyke, a quarter of the world's diamonds reserves, especially at our "Mai Mujuru's breast", in Chiadzwa, that would amount to 1.2 billion USA dollars per month. The simple question is; who will mine them when most of the mine companies in Zimbabwe are closing, in fact, who would like to mine for little peanuts they will get from the Reserve Bank, i.e. from Gono himself, and worse still, in the despised Zimbabwe dollars notes. Who would be willing to open a mine, which would later be confiscated by the government, considering the legislation of 51per cent indigenous ownership Mugabe signed onto law in the mining and industry field. I bet even the preferred Chinese wouldn't like the coin of this idea.

This kind of convoluted thinking is what worries all and sundry, and Tendai Biti and the MDC especially. The thinking, according to Biti, is saying, "We don't have to worry about Morgan Tsvangirai, the power sharing deal, the western world; we will get our money from the diamonds and commodities and forget the rest of them." Tendai Biti concludes that it is Gono at his best, that he is the mother and father of this disastrous kind of engineering. I said I would give Gono the benefit of doubt but with all these arguments it would be very difficult to do so. What decides me is that the article's recommendations were later adopted, and now Zimbabwe is unofficially using the Rand and the American dollar, and has also done away with the fickle Zimbabwe dollar.

But I feel this is all a case of too little too late. Multi-currency should have been adopted a long time ago (5 plus years ago before the inflation had become too rife). Instead of depending on printing bearer cheques and cutting zeroes that inversely pushed inflation up, we should have adopted these stable currencies a long time ago. But, as always, the fun thing with Zimbabwe is that once again it has happened in the lifetime of yet another, "It will never happen in my lifetime", person. These are the kind of tales that have become typical of Zimbabwe: a land of lost opportunities and dreamed gonoisms.

Dream on Zimbabwe!

There Is No Cholera in Zimbabwe

"Harare is sitting on a cholera time bomb, as the deadly disease, which has claimed the lives of more than 20 people in the capital's satellite town of Chitungwiza recently, is spreading fast" Stanley Gama, The Saturday Star, 4 October 2008. This is the title paragraph of a story I had read in October 2008. I had dismissed it then as another of those scare stories that newspaper journalist like to be the first ones to broach, but will later on fizzle into nothing much. But I should have known better, especially after the last year's episode. This was the last year's episode.

"I start feeling a little fun and like shit after our Sunday Mass at around ten mid-mornings. It is early November, in 2007. When I return home from the church I sleep a little bit, thinking that it is just a small ailment. When I wake up, in the early afternoons, I am feeling a little bit better. At about one o clock in the afternoon I accompany Tambudzai, a church mate, to the Church for the afternoon youth-group activities. I am still feeling a little bit groggy. Sometimes, I would feel some cold sizzling shivers trembling through my spine. Sometimes I have this funny headache, but I shrug these things off.

When I arrive home from the afternoon church I am really cold, shivering and feeling like vomiting. My stomach is an upheaval of some sort and by about eight at night it is full blown vomiting, and a running stomach. Instantly I become 'Toilet Express'. Mostly it is blood that I am letting loose from my bowels. This also means I have an infection in my stomach. The next day, I don't simply go to work, neither to the passport offices where I was processing my passport. The only strength I have is for me to make it to the toilet. I am like every 5 minutes or so I have to run to the toilet. Later, the same day, I take a couple of Cotri tablets which I got from my sister, Stella; who the previous week was infected but it hadn't been so bad with her.

The pills don't improve my situation. Going to the hospital is a waste of time because other people have gone there and returned back without not even a painkiller. But, of course, with the salt and sugar solution as the suggested remedy. The hospitals and clinics don't have any pills or medicine for cholera. This situation has been caused by the water we have been drinking, which is from ZINWA treatment works. Treatment of water had been removed from Harare city council authority by the government and ZINWA (Zimbabwe National Water Authority) had been formed by the government. It had been entrusted with the mandate to treat water and sell it directly to the customers. The government did this just to spite the opposition party, which won all the urban municipalities in the 2005 election. This organisation had failed miserably to provide clean water and the water we were getting was smelly greenish syrup. If you leave it in a glass, for a couple of minutes, half bottom of the glass will be filled up by some muddy, smudgy, darkish substance. It was obvious the water had too many E-coli bacteria, more than was normal for human consumption.

There is nowhere else we could get better water so we have to drink this water. The alternative was to fetch it straight from the river Hunyani, where this dirty water was coming from, or to dig wells in waterways around the city. These wells would, of course, be made up of water coming from the spewing sewage rivers all over the city, which were emptying into these waterways. The next day Kudzanai, my sister's little kid, enters the fray. It is now the two of us. The morrow day Kudzanai's mother, Judith, enters the race to the toilet and it becomes a three-some horse race.

I can't eat anything without vomiting it afterwards, but on Thursday I get a couple of tablets from my next-door neighbour, Mai Agnes. I don't even know the name of those tablets. That day, Kudzanai becomes fine, but my other two brothers, Lucky and George, also enter the race. It is minor with these two guys such that by the morrow day they are fine. We can't help joking and calling them Cholera 1 and Cholera 2, because of their Immunity to the disease. The morrow day my situation begins to improve, but Judith's situation is fast becoming severe. We are so afraid for her. This is exacerbated by her condition, for she has some sort of blood shortage situation such that losing blood is debilitating her severely.

By Thursday night she can't even walk but is now grovelling on all fours to the toilet. On Friday she is sleeping by the toilet's door. On Saturday our mother arrives from our rural home where she stays with our father but by then my condition had stabilized. I had thinned quite terribly. Not even a single one of my trousers could fit me without belting it tightly. I can't walk a distance of more than 5 metres without resting, but Judith's situation is still a cause for concern because she hasn't improved any.

On Sunday, I begin to eat without vomiting the food afterwards. The following day I go to the passport office in Harare and, later on; to my work place after failing to make any headway at the passport offices. I am applying for a passport. I want to leave the country for

South Africa. Going to work in Zimbabwe is now a wasteful exercise. What one gets paid doesn't even provide for a week's worth of food, let alone any other things necessary for a decent life. I have to put on some slippers and walk so slowly so as not to strain myself. When I arrive at my workplace they are shocked to find me that thinned. Some of my work friends can't help but tease me that I have HIV or AIDS, some not so joke-fully would watch me with faces that suggested that.

Judith later recovers. We are so lucky that nobody dies in our family but a lot of people die in the weeks preceding and after this, including my next-door neighbour, Sekuru Zengeza, who dies before seeing the New Year. Now, a year after all that, a lot of people are dying, all over the country, at a proportion that has never been seen before in Zimbabwe because of Cholera. Little did we know, back then, that it would come to this, some day?"

I have now been staying in South Africa. So when I read the Stanley Gama's story in the Saturday Star newspaper, I knew I was bit removed from the eye of the storm. There was little chance of me acquiring this disease again, but I was still afraid for my family in Zimbabwe. In Stanley Gama's story in The Saturday Star, he goes further on to say that many Zimbabweans were fleeing into South Africa from the crumbling economy, who may have the highly infectious disease, which spreads through unhygienic conditions, and was exacerbated by the collapse of the health delivery system in Zimbabwe.

It is a great wonder why Sikhanyiso Ndlovu, then Information and publicity minister, could sink so low as to suggest that it was Britain's biological warfare against Zimbabwe; suggesting that British agents

96

had poisoned Chitungwiza waters in order to create this human catastrophe, as an excuse to put pressure on, or to intervene in the internal affairs of Zimbabwe. It can only make me realise that the likes of Ndlovu have never walked the streets of any high density suburb in Zimbabwe in the last 5 years. Had he done that he could have seen sewage flowing all over Chitungwiza, little children playing in the sewer rivers, people fetching water from unprotected wells. He could also have seen non-availability of clean water, for weeks on end, in these high density suburbs; the failure of ZINWA to provide both Chitungwiza and Harare residents with clean water to drink. He could have simply figured out that all these had caused this contamination. But I am sure he knew of all this, even his boss Mugabe, with his insensitive jokes, "There is no cholera in Zimbabwe". In one of his campaign rallies at Chibuku stadium, in Chitungwiza, he also made a jibe at this place, and on us, when he said the place smells so bad, when referring to Chitungwiza. These two people knew about all this, but as always, it was just some sick political gamesmanship, as usual. But such insensitivity is galling, to say the least.

The disease would at least have been contained but due to lack of medicines in the hospitals it was being aggravated, with patients being ordered to look for medicines in pharmacies, which were almost devoid of supplies. When, and mostly in the rare cases, the medicines could be found in these pharmacies, the medicines would be so unaffordable to most people. Zimbabwe Lawyers for Human Rights blamed the government in a read speech. "The on-going deaths, a result of official and criminal negligence, have brought despair to the affected families and communities. It is alarming and quite unusual for such a preventable disease to continue to claim such valuable lives in this day and age." George Charamba, Mugabe's spokesperson hit back at Mugabe, at the British, and I should think at their hated cousins, the Americans, and the cholera victims by saying Mugabe was only joking, making some jokes at the British, and this is the joke he was making.

Suppose your wife, child, husband, family member, or friend has been shot dead in cold blood, pre-meditated shooting. Then the person who has killed them tells you that they are not dead because nobody killed them. Yet you know there are dead and you have buried them and some are still to be buried. I suppose this is the joke that Mugabe was making when he said, "There is no cholera in Zimbabwe".

Friday, December 17, 2010 (a diary extract from, IT'S NOT ABOUT ME.)

Late last night we were talking with my sister, Judith, about the cholera of 2008-2009. It started the conversation: my little nephew Kudzanai had been catching ant-flies (Ishwa) for consumption for some days. He was keeping them in a cup, dead or alive; unseasoned at that. Some of which were now rotting. He wanted to roast and consume them and was building a sizable portion for a sizable meal. But, I forcefully took them away from him and threw them in the toilet and flushed them. At first the mother didn't like that, but she later realised why I did that. So, we started talking with my sister, the mother of Kudzanai, of the cholera. She told me that our cousin had also died from that cholera epidemic. In total, in the recorded cases, it gobbled over 5 000 people, but of course, it could be 2 or 3 times more than that. It was my first time hearing of it; that cousin Michael was dead. She also told me that over twenty people had died in our little village, Mapfurira village, in Nyanga, Nyatate, where we grew up

98

some many moons ago. I am sure all these deaths were not even part of the recorded 5 000 dead. It devastated me greatly. I can't even get around to the idea that Cousin Michael (Mukoma Maikoro, as we affectionately called him) has been dead and buried in the soils for two years now, and that I had been thinking he was still alive.

I had always been very close to Mukoma Maikoro when we were growing up. He was one hell of a great friend and family maker. He used to visit our family several times in a week. Such an affable man he was. It reminds me of when we were little, before we had started going to school, late seventies or early eighties, thereabouts. We would stay with our grandma Helen those days, my father's mother. Momma was in Harare with father where my father worked so that the two of us, me and my brother Bernard, were left in the care of grandma. One day Mukoma Maikoro came over to our household and we were having tea with yams. It was our favourite morning meal, and it still is my favourite. Instead of waiting to be given his share, he took my own portions. I howled in tears but he just bowled over in laughter and ate them anyway, without a care as to my tears. Then, I didn't like him but I have grown to like him, quite a lot over the years.

We always could spend unaccounted hours arguing about life, religion or anything else worth fighting over. But it was mostly about religion. He was of the apostolic sect, Johann Marange apostolic church. Their religion believed prayers were the only cure or solution to every cause, disease and trouble, or everything else. He believed in that fervently. I didn't think, and I still don't think medicines for the cure of disease is unimportant. Mukoma Maikoro, I suppose, had to hold firm to his beliefs, that it was only prayers that could heal diseases and paid the price of his beliefs; together with the other twenty or so apostolic sect members. It's so disheartening, but I believe he is happy where he is. He was happy here on earth, so he should be happy?

South Africa vs. The United Nations

Lawrence Caromba, of the Centre for International Political Studies, at the University of Pretoria, feels that South Africa's tenure at the Security Council has been a "foreign policy disaster." He feels that instead of advancing its multilaterism goals, it has bloated its human rights copy book by voting for dictators like Mugabe and the Myanmar generals. Caromba believes South Africa's multilaterism has a slightly different goal; to thwart the 5 permanent members of the Security Council. I would like to add that, especially the USA and UK, so that South Africa usually has aligned itself with China or Russia and thereby correct what South Africa feels is a global power imbalance. Caromba and many others feels that this rather nebulous and unrealistic goal is hardly a price worth to pay for, in lost reputation and spoiled relations with especially the world's superpower, the USA. He thinks that South Africa should have joined the USA in voting for the United Nations Security Council resolution to impose sanctions on Mugabe, to pressure him to make concessions during the negotiations process

Is South Africa trying to be a strategic rival to the USA?

NO! According to Pretoria; Pretoria posits that the African union is opposed to sanctions against Mugabe, in trying to avoid upsetting Mugabe and Mbeki's mediation processes, thus South Africa is just obeying orders from its bosses. According to Peter Fabricius in The Star, of August 1 2008, this argument neglects South Africa's wider obligation to the United Nations Security Council, who are South

Africa's real bosses. The United Nations Security Council mandate is to act in the best interest of mankind, wherever in the world- that is including the victims of Mugabe's violence. Fabricius also draws a parallel with the Al Bashir resolution which South Africa, Libya and other Arab countries are strongly opposed to, against the USA and UK who are trying to get the council to pass a resolution which would enable the International Criminal Court(ICC) to indict Al Bashir for war crimes in Darfur. South Africa wants an African court, or even at that, a Sudanese court to try him rather than the ICC, who it feels is picking on African leaders only.

But, how likely it is that a Sudanese court would conduct a fair and fearless trial against its leader, ask Fabricius?

What does the Darfur victims or Zimbabwe victims want?
Nobody seems to care.

This South African government is a big hypocrite. It is always ranging about Israel but ups the tyranny of Mugabe. It opposes the UN Security Council resolution on Zimbabwe, Darfur, Burma but wax lyrical about Bush's war on Iraq. Max Du Preez feels, and rightly so, that this has been the problem with our continent since the days tyrant and mass murderer Idi Amin was cheered at meetings of the old Organisation of African unity.

"As a continent we fear and honour the violent dictates among us in the name of African pride and solidarity" says Max Du Preez, The Star, 29 January 2009. Du Preez is ashamed that an ANC leader has been a part of this African charade, not just one but now two leaders.

Is the Security Council having excessive powers?

South Africa tenure as the chairman of the United Nations Security Council has now ended on 31 December 2008, and it was fraught with the thinking that the United Nations Security Council is a rogue elephant that grinds developing countries by getting involved in the internal affairs of these countries. So, South Africa dedicated its time as the chairman at the Security Council to curb this marauding animal. But international law expert Hans Winkler, who is a former minister in the Australian government, offers a different perspective. "I don't think you can find a single case where the Security Council authorised force illegally...but you can name a dozen cases where it didn't act but should have." Fabricius, in another article in The Star, of March 6 2009, also feels that the essential question that should be considered was not how to stop the Security Council exceeding its powers, but how to ensure it did not shirk from exercising the powers it ought to. Consider what the situation would have been like if it had exercised its powers in the DRC, Rwanda, Burundi, and Bosnian genocides.

In 2005, the UN membership adopted the responsibility to protect doctrine and this gave the UN the responsibility to intervene, if human rights abusers like Mugabe and Al Bashir take upon themselves as their right to abuse their citizens, or do not want to stem abuse in their countries when they have the powers to do so. Historically, the UN has moved from the initial function as a political body resolving specific disputes, and usually there were between countries. Now it is the world's legislator, judge, and executor, that is; it can pass general laws, set up complex regimes of sanctions and measures, and create several tribunes like the ICC, so that it can act

103

swiftly and decisively. It could be because of this that South Africa feels it has grown too big, and has all the powers of governance and that no other organisation is there to neutralise its powers.

The other thinking that has been entrenched in the minds of developing countries, on this body's functions, especially stems from the Veto powers that some countries have, and this has been in discussions since the mid-1990s by the African leaders. They feel and have resolved that they want the UN Security Council to be reformed and either absolve the Veto powers. Alternatively, to include some more countries, especially developing countries, to have these veto powers in Africa, Central and Latin America, and Asia; so that their voices could be heard. But if it is for this that Africa and South Africa blocked the UN resolution on Zimbabwe, then it still feels like whatever powers Africa wants, would be for the leaders to protect themselves, not for empowering the breath of Africa's citizens.

The United Nations Security Council has to embark on reforms and should spread the powers it has from the 5 permanent members, especially from the USA and UK's control, or to simply dissolve this post-First World War Security Council, and create another one, or maybe; to alternatively depend on the general assembly, for decision-making since this body represents the entire world. Some matters should be spread out, by giving executive powers to relevant bodies of the UN to deal with issues relevant to them, like the ICC, UNHCR, and the Human Rights Council. And before passing a resolution, it should ensure that all those that are its targets have been given the right to a fair hearing.

I feel it is not right thinking to redress some of the above issues, by blocking the UN from executing its fundamental function so as to make it adopt these reforms, rather countries like South Africa should have been at the forefront to ensure that the UN has done its job: that of, "The protector", in Zimbabwe.

Chinese Imperialism for Political Protection?

China-Africa trade has surged by an average 30per cent a year this decade, soaring to nearly $107 billion dollars in 2008 and Chinese companies have pledged tens of billions to Africa in loans, and investments to secure raw materials for its burning bright economy. You can talk of interest in the Zambian copper belt, the Standard bank in South Africa, oil in Angola, Hauwei technologies in North Africa, Bong iron ore deposit in Liberia, infrastructure development and investment projects in DRC, Beling iron ore development in Gabon, and the list is endless. Made in China products have flooded every African country, products that are substandard, in fact, third level quality, by Chinese quality standards. The products are affordable to African countries, so that China's exports to Africa have gone up 40per cent to $23 billion dollars year-on-year in the first half of 2008. Most of the small business offices spaces in Harare, many parastatals, many mines, farms etc, have Chinese presence in their shareholding in Zimbabwe.

Against this backdrop, suppose a country like Zimbabwe, Sudan, and the DRC is brought before the Security Council for gross-abuse of its citizen's rights, do you think China would trouble itself by protecting the human rights of these citizens, when it knows that by so doing, it would incur the displeasure of the leaders of these countries? China has always protected its interests in Africa, by torpedoing any sanction resolution brought on any country it feels it has interests in. Like the America that we have come to know! It doesn't only do that in Africa but even in Asia like in North Korea, the Middle East or South America. As the whole world, particularly most of the resource rich developing countries tries to do away with American imperialism they are doing this by substituting it with Chinese imperialism. Like the old African saying, "we struggle very hard to remove one cockroach from power and the next rat comes to do the same thing", this is the sad truth of our continent.

Wona Katerere

I really love to be me; I am Wona Katerere. The first child of the governor of Harare province, what a catch! I demand to be sent to the best schools in the country. I always choose huge schools like the Franciscan convent. I like it very much there because it's right in the middle of the capital city. I don't really feel abandoned. I don't want to go to some boarding school in the middle of the bushes, somewhere in the nowhere of the rural areas, no. Franciscan convent is a super school run by the Franciscans. I like those sisters so much. I know by choosing this school, it pleases my father no end. I still want him to think that I am still so pious of mind, so sweet and chaste like it's taught at the Catholic Church, which my father has been a member of all his life. It pleases him no end. I can't tell him kissing is, even at that, old news to me now. I have done it with an assortment of my guards. He should have seen how it drives them so crazy, knowing that they were bedding the child of the governor.

I like it very much at Franciscan convent. No little boy would try to grab me there. It's nice to know that I am forbidden territory to those fumbling dark knees school boys, but so warm and sweet to old man, who are husbands and experienced lovers and mature. I get it like a wife. I demand more. It's cool, really. I don't care about grades here. They would have to give me better grades if they don't want to incur my father's wrath again. They don't want another scene with the governor of Harare, not another one, no. They once tried to fight my father over my school fees but my father told them he was going to pay the gazetted fee; gazetted, of course, by the minister of education or else he would have the school closed.

We called him "The goat", the minister of education, even my father always laughed at him saying he was taking the education of the country back to the Middle Ages. The good thing is my father can always get us, his children, to the few good schools in the country. The Goat, at one time, wanted to retire from being a minister to become a chief in the bloody dusty bowls of the rural areas. That's our minister, someone who thinks he is more qualified as a traditional chief, and then; he also shocked the entire nation when he suggested he wanted to create one school uniform for the whole country, making the entire country into one school. Just think of that!

The sisters had whined to no end; saying that exclusive schools always charged higher fees to cater for the quality education which was given at those schools and the superb conditions, and the blah bah blah other things. My father would imitate them in a funny sort of way that would make us howl with laughter at home. My father insisted on paying the gazetted fee or he would have the school closed immediately by the minister. The sisters obliged. I didn't care about the whole situation, really. I only wanted to be at this school. My father didn't care either about the fact that this school had other expenses that it had to meet, like sourcing and paying for quality teachers who had to be paid better salaries than C-class schools. That, these A-class schools, especially boarding schools had to provide better accommodation, food, classes, and other facilities; even better books, laboratories and extra curriculum activities than the C–class schools. He didn't care and I didn't care either.

It makes me think a little bit about some secondary schools, the class schools dotted all over the country where; over half of the teachers were unqualified ordinary secondary school certificates holders, where the grounds were dusty uneven bowls, where the library had just some few books that one could finish reading in one school term, where the classrooms were substandard, where you would sit on the benches rather than chairs for nearly 8 hours a day, where the entire school had to share one laboratory room, where you didn't even have the privilege of being a boarding student, where you could only access ZIMSEC (Zimbabwe Schools Examination Council) certificates, not Cambridge education, and the list is endless. Come to think of it, I can't even overlook the fact that where the only punishment was corporal punishment. I saw one of those schools in the undeveloped northern parts of the country when I was with my father on the campaign trail last year. I can't even think of myself going to such a school.

It's not only my father who is getting his kids in these classy schools so I don't see what the fuss is all about. All his cronies in the ruling party are paying peanuts in whatever A-class schools their kids are in all over the country, but getting world class Cambridge education and certificates. No one makes such a huge fuss about it. This year when the schools were closed due to the bungling of the education system by the Goat, we didn't close at the Convent. I heard that even for the general people to have their kids in these schools they had to be members of the ruling party, well known members, and such was the situation that even when one could afford the fees, he had to be a well-known leader of the party to have their children getting places at these schools. It's not my father who put that law; maybe it's the Goat, so people shouldn't blame my father for all that, as well.

This same thing happened with the farms and everyone blamed my father, rather than those hordes of the ruling party's bigwigs who got all the best farms. My father didn't get many farms; just a couple of Zishungo farms. The rest of the farms they say my father owns are for my cousins and relatives, not my father. The majority of the people were given sandy, shallow farms; which couldn't even sustain any crops, so also is the education situation now. Why is my father being blamed for that? Not the Goat or that woman MP who owns over seven farms. Seven farms she doesn't even utilize! At least my father supplies milk, half of the country's milk wants, on just two Zishungo farms.

When I finish my Cambridge "A" levels, I don't want to go to any university in the country. There is not much learning happening at those universities; there are no lecturers anywhere in the country. I have already gotten a place at Shanghai University. I wanted to go to the UK or to an Australian university but after that last year's debacle of those two ruling party's children. My father said he didn't want to be humiliated like that. Australia had set precedence the previous year when it deported 8 students of ruling party leaders. My father was afraid that the whole of the western world would follow suit. Australia highhandedly deported those children, saying it wanted to prevent those involved in human rights abuses in the country from giving their children education denied to ordinary people, and other blah bah, blahs... who really cares?

I have to make the most of my staying away from my family in China, really. I will party like you have never seen it. Shanghai is fine by me; at least there is no cholera there. Here, people are wasting away and dying from cholera, or the said to be "There is no cholera in ...." disease. He is so good at deflecting pressure of himself; my

111

father is also that good. We were so concerned that my father was losing his job over that cholera thing, a couple of months ago, when the whole world made a lot of noise about our shopping trip to China. They were saying we were wasting the money that should have been put to use, in treating these cholera patients as if we had spent quite a lot of money at that; as if we had caused that cholera on these people. It was only some couple of thousands of dollars after all. Ok, it was just 72 000 dollars. It's not a lot of money as compared to what other children and wives of politicians spent on shopping sprees in Paris and other European capitals. Maybe they wanted us to spend that money in European cities, but they banned us from going there?

At least Shanghai University doesn't have to prove to anyone and vouchsafe that whatever monies that my father uses to pay for my fees was not looted from the country. I don't give a fig about ordinary children of ordinary people, ordinary what! They don't deserve to get the same education that Shanghai University would offer me. They have to be responsible for what members of their families did? That is, angering my father by trying to remove him from power by a pen rather than by a sword. The irony of it all is that, education and a pen go hand in hand. The western nations are also making us pay by banning us from going there for shopping trips for the purported sins of our father, so it's fair that they should suffer, as well. They might as well go and shop in London, these stupid ordinary people and their stupid children, really! Oh! Even their favoured western nations have cut them out of the possibilities of getting scholarships for study abroad. They can't even be considered for the Commonwealth scholarships; even the high handed Australians haven't included them on consideration for the Ausaid scholarships. Let them go and rot at Lupane University or the University of Zimbabwe, for all that I care!

Hunger Strike

"In 1981, Northern Ireland's Bobby Sands used the non-violent tactic of the hunger strike successfully to evoke public interest and support." The Star, Jan 22 2009. He was supporting the Northern Ireland independence from Britain. I remember growing up hearing of it being referred to as the "Irish question" or issue, and the Sein Fein was the party that had the Irish republican army, which Bobby Sands was the first of its 10 provisional volunteers to die in prison on May 5 1981, on his 66th day of his fast. On the news, especially in the 1990s, we grew up with news of the IRA's bombings of southern Belfast and London. Their leader, Gerry Adams, featured a lot in the news. Mahatma Ghandi really had a go at this form of protest earlier on, and successfully influenced the ouster of British colonialism in India, and stopped his countrymen from killing each other, as well.

Here is a story that happened to me and my family, about the mid-1980s. We had a maid and a general hand, Florence and Lovemore. All of Florence's clothes and a couple of our things were stolen when we had gone to the church. When we returned home from church we looked for these things, all around our village, even asking some people. Some people said they had seen Lovemore with the suitcase full of things. The descriptions fitted that of Florence's suitcase. Lovemore had been fired recently by my mother for non-performance of his duties, and as well, for drunkenness and rowdy behaviour. Back then, my family believed in the consultations of N'angas (the traditional healers) and faith healers, so they consulted a faith healer who told my mother that we had to fast for seven days,

114

eating only one meal per day, at after six in the evenings and, to pray, as well. That, during the fasting time we didn't have to drink water but the prescribed blue sulphate solution. We had to also bath in water steaming so hot, after immersing two very hot stones and the sulphate solution into it. This prophet consecrated these things (the stones and the sulphate solution), and said that we would have our things before the expiry of the seven days' fast.

Into fasting we entered, and it was so painful for me and my brother, since deep down we didn't believe this faith healer. That week was one hell of a time for us. Some other times, when we couldn't take it anymore, we would sneak behind mother and eat whatever food we knew was lying somewhere, unknown by our mother. But, even at that, when we had our meals at night, we demanded for and ate everything we had forgone in the morning and afternoon. Having to eat all that, at the same time, was a painful thing to do and it would take a lot of time for us to deal with the effects of bloated stomachs. We hated this. What galled us to distraction was the sulphate solution that we had to drink. It was so smelly that by about the day's end, of our first day of fasting, it was all that we could smell. It also rattled insidiously in our stomachs.

When fasting ended on the seventh day, we managed to find a couple of our things, in fact, my brother's bookcase and some books, just some distances from our homes, at a point we would pass through several times that week without seeing them. We never could find Florence's things. My parents had to later on buy her the things and sent them to her relatives, where she was now staying after resigning from our place. We both liked her so much, me and my brother, in fact, I was secretly in love with her. I think that kind of love a boy at puberty stage would have for an older girl. We had to go through all that especially for her, but in the end, I hated the idea of having to be forced to fast again. I have never had to fast for over a day after that for I think I like my food so much as to forgo it for that much longer again.

Later on, I read in the bible a verse on fasting which was later explained to me by my Parish Priest, Father Timothy Fives, at my local parish, St Agnes Catholic Church, Zengeza, which galvanised my beliefs on fasting. God says in the verse that what he wants from us is love, not fasting. Something like that! What you have to do is to love him, to love others, to love yourself, before praying, before fasting, and when you fast it should come from your heart. I also realised it's not only food that you can fast with. With that in mind, it makes me think what if the whole of South Africa were to fast on Zimbabwe's problems by refusing, or abstaining from doing any form of trade with the despotic regime in Zimbabwe. I mean the entire South African society enforcing this on its government, to show their fellow feeling and love of their neighbours up north. It's a hard call and thought.

Getting to the gist of this article, the non-governmental organisations, churches and other civic organisations launched their own brand of the hunger strikes, against the despotic regime in Zimbabwe. Some of the organisations participating are Civicus, Zimbabwe Solidarity Forum, Crisis in Zimbabwe Coalition, Solidarity Peace Trust and Foundations for Human Rights, lead among others by Sipho Theys, Elinor Sisulu, Selvan Chetty, Yasmin Sooka, Kumi Naidoo (who started the fasting) and Nomboniso Gasa. The campaign aims to mobilise the support and solidarity of South Africans, to urge their government to show more urgency in solving the Zimbabwean crisis. Before that Nobel Prize winner, archbishop emeritus Desmond Tutu, and I have to admit I admire this old wiser. The hell-riser had started fasting, at least once per week, in solidarity with the people of Zimbabwe.

When I heard of all this and applied it to me and my feelings against fasting, I couldn't help being sceptical. I said "no, not fasting again, no." It was my suppressed reaction.

Undoing Mugabe

1 .The way he treated Matabeleland people in the 1980's saw the seeds of distrust. Even when he had stifled Nkomo enough, into agreeing on the power sharing government in 1987, the people in Matebeleland still remained with unhealed scars and wounds. They were waiting, all these years, for an opportunity to fight him and do away with him. When the MDC came about they more easily adopted it than other rural provinces. It was this distrust that the people from Matabeleland had for Mugabe, and later on for Nkomo and ZAPU, for joining Mugabe, that could be the reason why even after the other former ZAPU cadres had re-formed the ZAPU party that it still has failed to make any in roads, for some time, into this explosive area.

2. In 1987 Mugabe was given executive powers in the Edson Zvobgo inspired and drafted constitution, but Mugabe has misused these executive powers over the years, to silence the people's displeasure with his governance and any opposition against his rule. He came hard on civil protest, made redundant political rivals, such that ordinary people in Zimbabwe began to be too aware, too early, of Mugabe's autocratic tendencies. That's why, just after 10 years of his rule, Zimbabwe Unity Movement (ZUM), and Tekere made a lot of noise in the 1990 general election. It was a mirror into the people's increasing displeasure with their leader, whom they had voted for overwhelmingly in the previous 2 elections periods (1980, 1985).

3. Mugabe's particular favouritism of Mashonaland and Masvingo leaders, and in so doing, he has isolated leaders and people from other provinces, especially those from Manicaland and Matabeleland. These people and, the leaders from these provinces felt alienated from the political and economic landscape and destiny of Zimbabwe, by the Zezuru-Karanga alliance and later on, by the Zezuru-Karanga-Ndebele tripartite ruling class. Canaan Banana, Mugabe, Simon Muzenda, Joshua Nkomo, Joseph Msika, Joyce Mujuru, and even the national chairman of ZANUPF, Joseph Nkomo, all have been from these ruling alliances and tribal areas. This has always galvanised Manicaland people to fight against this dominance and alienation by the Zezuru-Karanga alliance, especially in the Shona provinces and social landscape. It was for this dominance by the Shona people that Ndebele people also fought Mugabe. It is the dominance of the Manicaland people by the Zezuru-Karanga groups that they have always supported their sons, especially if there were rebelling against Mugabe's leadership style.

That's the reason why even though Tsvangirai had not come through this province's ZANUPF leadership structures, people in Manicaland easily identified with him more than any other Shona political provinces. They took to him as their own son for he is originally from Buhera, which is in the political province of Manicaland. It took the other Shona provinces like the Mashonaland and Masvingo provinces, up to 10 years to start embracing him.

4. Corruption in the government ministries and department's over the years was another of Mugabe's undoing. Way back, in the late 1980's, ructions from corruption by ministers were felt all over the country and abroad, especially after the Judge Wilson Sandura spearheaded hearings into Willowvale Mazda Motor Industries'

119

vehicles scandal(the Willogate scandal), that embroiled ministers like Enos Nkala, Enoch Dumbusthena, and Morris Nyagumbo, and even the presidium itself. This resulted in Nyagumbo committing suicide, or being killed, whichever way you might look at it, to abscond from being jailed. It is also this job that put to halt Sandura's career as a judge. Ever since his fine works on this scandal he has always been overlooked for appointments, in favour of government apologists. This corruption trial made a lot of noise and made people in Zimbabwe to be aware of the fact that their elected government was corruptive.

Ever since that, over the years, this ruling coterie has been embroiled in one scandal after another. Like Mobuto's government in Zaire, this government slashed billions of donor aid money and loans, even funds meant to finance governance itself, such that the government became ineffective in doing its job. This crash, grab and run mentality was adopted throughout the social fabric of Zimbabwe. Board of directors, senior management, middle managers, and line managers adopted these corruptive tendencies into the public and private sectors and government institutions. Rural authorities, urban authorities, workers and even NGO's all took to this grab mentality. Corruption permeated every level of the society, and even moralist would preach about corruption and moral re-generation with their mouths whilst their hands were slashing billions into their accounts. All this could only lead to failure of the government, industry, organisations and institutions of social service. One after the other they folded or became dysfunctional.

The poor ordinary people, though they were very much part of this grab, could not change their conditions through this grab, because they grabbed very little away from the powerful who grabbed a lion's

120

share. These poor people ended up even more poorer, envious, jealous and hard done by the powerful; so the only way that these people could come to terms and at par with the powerful people was to dislodge the powerful people from their enriching positions. I am saying; to say that corruption was only confined to the upper echelons of our society is to miss the whole point. Everyone in Zimbabwe became corruptive, one way or another, for it became the only way to survive at that time. But still, the blame of the emergency of this pestilence lies squarely on the government's shoulders and Mugabe.

5. Whilst we are still on a related topic, I feel the black market (informal market) was a response from the downtrodden against the government leaders' "have it all", grab and attitude. People who couldn't find jobs, people who felt their jobs had become useless and couldn't afford them some basic necessities, people who felt they could also become rich and powerful, like some government leaders, through this dealing on the black market, invaded this market. The black market became the only way to survive. Even those who still could keep to their jobs kept them, but also doubled up by doing a bit of selling and buying on this black market.

A friend of mine I worked with went to Mozambique every end of every month to buy some basic commodities for consumption, and for selling throughout the month. Another work-mate who was part of management could just come to work a couple of hours, or do an hour's work per day, but most of the times he would be busy running his own farm and private businesses. He used the company's resources to further his private businesses like the telephones, companies' computers, fax, photocopying machines, company car, fuel, and other allowances.

121

This strong black market drove the economy to hyper-inflation, coupled with the non-performance of the formal industry, and for years Gono, the Reserve bank governor, and Leonard Tshumba before him, failed to deal with this informal market. This informal market later spawned into fuel hoarding, foreign currency hoarding and still later, cash hoarding, even in formal banks. There is a time when Gono changed the bearer cheques, but before they even were circulating to the public, over 10 billion of those bearer cheques were already in the informal hands. The woman who was caught with these bearer cheques confessed that she had got them from some senior Reserve bank boss and government officials. This ended up implicating a ZANUPF official, who absconded from arrest and prosecution by debunking to the UK. There was even talk of Gono's involvement in dealing in this informal market. Another story was of how many other government officials had become involved in this market, such that the much needed foreign currency needed for running the government and for imports were being stashed into off-shore accounts by these ZANUPF bigwigs like Makamba, Kuruneri, to mention just a few. Every senior government employee, it seemed, had or has a stashed foreign off-shore account, and I remain to be disproved on this assertion.

The black market did not contribute to the country's tax and fiscus base. The government did not get anything from it, yet it was the driving engine of the economy and country. The total effect of this informal market was to make governance impossible. This is one of the most important undoing of Mugabe, for he lost total control of the economy, and programmes like the Reserve bank's inspired Operation Sunrise and also the government's Operation Murambatsvina were an uninformed response against this scourge.

6. ESAP (Economic Structural Adjustment Programme) subjected to the Zimbabweans, with the blind acceptance of this by the government, by the International Monetary Fund, and The World Bank, in the late 1980's up to the middle 1990's. Whilst this programme helped in structuring government and companies' expenditure, it did not create jobs for ordinary people but left a lot of people jobless, neither did it create wealth for them, but rather it made the ordinary people the poorer; and the industry and foreign individuals who controlled those industries, richer. The ordinary people held the government responsible for forcing this ESAP on them and for its effects. I remember Bernard Chidzero, who was the finance minister then, and who devised this programme with the help of the IMF and the World Bank; used to be derided by ordinary people for this ESAP programme. It used to be referred to as "VaChidzero's ESAP", even by Mugabe himself and the ordinary people. By the time the government managed to do away with it, the economy had been knocked hard, and as well, the people by this ESAP programme. The government was distrusted by its citizens, especially its growing educated citizens who were mostly in urban communities.

7. This half cooked up economic programme was later on watered down into another half-baked one and another... Remembering all their names, ever afterwards, even those before this one, is like an exercise into trying to figure out the thinking of the person who imposed these programmes on his people. All these programmes did not improve the lot of the people. They became a pointer, on the inability of our government to run competently our country and the economy, and inversely, most of these programmes destroyed industry as company after company downsized, closed, or relocated.

By about mid1990's workers were getting a raw deal out of all this. This gave rise to Union strikes, and later, national strikes; and these strikes also destroyed the economy all the more because some of these strikes became an opportunity of looting and vandalization. I must admit they were a few people in Harare and Chitungwiza who would say they never looted something or another during those strikes. Another effect was the loss in productive work that these massive strikes caused on industry and ultimately on the government in lost tax. The total effect was a hard knock on the industry, government, and the people.

8. In 1997, against every sane advice, Mugabe decided to unilaterally invade the DRC to help Laurent Kabila to fight the rebels who were on the outskirts of the capital, Kinshasa; from the hot spot of the eastern DRC. Zimbabwe, with a little help from Angola and Namibia, entered into this excursion, unbudgeted and unbeneficial to its citizens. Mostly, it must have been to secure the ruling party leaders' interests in the DRC from falling into the hands of the rebels. These top officials had diamond mining interests in the DRC. This unbudgeted war was said to have gobbled over 10 million United States dollars per month in reserves. This burn into our foreign currency reserves whittled our reserves from three months to a total deficit. The Zimbabwean dollar crashed. This ushered in our financial and economic problems and by the time the war was over we had lost our financial muscle. Mugabe had lost a lot of respect from his peers like Mandela, Obasanjo, and Masire who were against this excursion. Support from the donors and traditional financiers like IMF, UK, USA, France, and The World Bank dwindled. Money started drying up from our coffers. Mugabe also lost a lot of support from his own people.

9. His next bungling was when Mugabe gave the war veterans an unbudgeted Z$50 billion dollars pension and monthly stipends. This weakened our country's financial muscle just like the DCR venture. To pay up for this overture, the war veterans were organised into a formidable force and ultimately were thrown onto the white farmers and opposition members, whom Mugabe had lost love for. I have dealt with some of his reasons for attacking this group in other pieces, *Farm Invasion Episode; Rantings of a Raving Pen.* In so doing, Mugabe destroyed the agricultural sector and industry. White farmers re-located out of the country, and for the record over 100 of these farmers are in the Manica province of Mozambique alone. They left with their monies and expertise and this also raised the stakes for the democratic struggles and political manoeuvrings between Mugabe and Tsvangirai, the UK, USA, and most of the western world.

10. In 1999, the MDC was conceived by labour and civil society, through the backing of western donors and governments like the UK's West Minister Fund, and later the USA's Zimbabwe Democracy and Economic Recovery Act. This support made the MDC stronger financially. The government's previous bungling, some of which I have outlined above, made it easier for the MDC to tape into this "disillusioned with Mugabe" electorate. Within three months of its formation the MDC, together with the civil society like the NCA (National Constitutional Assembly,) defeated the government in the constitution amendment referendum of February 2000. They campaigned for the electorate to vote for a No-vote.

Why did I vote for this No-vote? One might say it was a political decision why a lot of people voted for a No-vote. The constitution had been written by well-trained people, some of them were Harvard graduates. I don't know whether being a Harvard graduate would give you much added right to be respected, even if you have created a no event constitution. The constitution had the same problems as the previous constitution (inspired and drafted by another former Harvard student, Edison Zvobgo). The executive powers! It is for this, or against this, that I voted for a No-vote, so did a lot of people. When people were saying they wanted the executive powers to be spread out, to be diluted from one pillar of government, and then they realised that nothing much had been done to that effect, it was easy to influence people not to endorse that constitution. The original constitution presented to Mugabe by the drafters, who also included a lot of MPs from the ZANUPF, could have been supported by the people if it had passed through the presidency, but Mugabe cut the part where his executive powers had been watered down a bit, and returned most, if not all, the executive powers he had in the 1987 constitution, and then added a very contentious issue, that of the land reform act. This incensed the Zimbabweans, and this resulted in the defeat of the constitution, by the people in a 55per cent versus 45per cent vote against the constitution.

And also, in 5 months of its birth, the MDC almost wrestled parliament from ZANUPF, in the 2000 elections. This scared the hell out of Mugabe and, like a haunted animal; he went into overdrive in order to protect his political life. His leadership, from that time onwards, became one of bungling, one of the destruction of opposition against him, one of utter dismay to the electorate, one of utter madness, one of an episode, one after another. The Zimbabweans, one after another, took up as their own right, the removal of this raging maniac out of Zimbabwe's political space. Even people from his own party, like Dzikamai Mavhaire, started the drive known as "Mugabe must go." Such was the dislike of Mugabe that was now ensconced into the Zimbabweans from all walks of life. Whilst people were going for this drive, Mugabe hit back, even a lot harder.

11. After the 2000 elections which Mugabe had thugged into victory, Britain especially galvanised the EU, and into drive they also entered and slapped Mugabe and his cronies in 2001 with targeted sanctions. It was political gamesmanship for the UK, USA, and most of the western world countries to maintain that the sanctions were only travel or targeted sanctions, targeted on Mugabe and his government. The truth is they became broad based sanctions as every donor, every major investor, every fund scurried out of the country. The far-reaching consequences of these sanctions were not only felt by Mugabe but mostly by the ordinary mass. The idea from Britain, especially, was to turn the people against their government, through this economic sabotage and warfare. The chief architect of this drive was Tony Blair, the UK prime minister. One can't help saying that if the USA were on the front paddle, the Americans, especially George Bush, could simply have bombed Mugabe out of Zimbabwe's political framework. But the British, especially Blair, used this blood-less warfare.

Even later on, when Blair tried to keep a blind eye on Zimbabwe, he was nudged into focusing onto it by his people. The opposition Conservative Party, now headed by the hot-air David Cameroon (which during Thatcher's and Major's years was rather tolerant and protective of Mugabe) also put pressure on Blair to solve the Zimbabwean issue. If there was one single outside influence that really troubled Mugabe, and also was most hated by Mugabe, it is Britain and Blair. Britain financed the Security Council sanctions, piled diplomatic pressure, supported every dissent against Mugabe, and made the right noises for most of the times, isolated Mugabe from one summit onto another, ate into the ZANUPF organisation through, for instance, Philip Chiyangwa's espionages for the British into the ZANUPF. Like a bullet head, Britain spearheaded the democratic struggle from the front of the muzzle. So did the USA, especially through their Zimbabwe Democracy and Economic Recovery Act, and its ambassador to Zimbabwe, Christopher Dell, whom Mugabe used to refer to as Christopher Hell. Australia, New Zealand, Canada, and even South Africa, though reluctantly so, listened to the British, so did the entire European Union, whose countries all helped Britain by putting pressure on Zimbabwe and applying the sanctions.

12. Technical skills as well as financial skills left the country, and were lost mostly to the countries mentioned above. Skills ranging from Andy Flower in cricket who left for the UK, to Mtuli Ncube (former Time bank owner, now Wits university head of the Business school), to Justice Paradza (whom I believe is now a professor at Auckland university), to Strive Masiyiwa (Econet owner who re-located to South Africa). This affected the competitiveness and viability of the Zimbabwean industry. In December 2007 alone, Australian telecommunication companies did interviews for technical skills jobs in Musina and Beitbridge, and took over 200 skilled workers, especially from the government's owned PTC, and this brought the PTC to its knees.

13. One operation after another, like operation Murambatsvina (operation clean-up), operation Zuva rabuda (operation sunrise), operation Makayiwana kupi (where did you get your wealth), operation Makavhotera papi (where and whom did you vote for), operation Bvisai mega (operation remove your own your satellite

dishes), and many others, were ill conceived ideas by Mugabe to stifle dissent against his rule, and were seen by ordinary Zimbabweans as autocratic acts that denied them of their rights.

14. Mugabe also tried to stifle dissent through Jonathan Moyo's inspired madness; when Jonathan Moyo went for both the print and electronic Medias, stifling them. The government also threatened the private Medias, through bombings of buildings of the Daily news, and the torture of journalists like Jeff Nyarota and Trevor Ncube. Chinamasa also entered the fray and made, and pushed for laws to muzzle dissent, such that even the NGO's, activists and opposition members got to the receiving end of these laws. Laws like AIPPA, POSA, and others were passed to kill off opposition against Mugabe. These muzzling were seen by ordinary people as an affront to their right to choose whom to govern them in a free and fair way.

15. The more the government tried to muzzle the people the more they fought back, and also the more a lot of people left the country for freer societies. When I started staying in South Africa I was surprised to find out that Zimbabwean issues were more covered than some important South African issues, even Zuma's trials were at par on coverage with the Zimbabwean issue. One could have been excused for thinking Zimbabwe is a very important province of South Africa (yes, it is a very important country to South Africa. We are South Africa's biggest trading partner on the African continent). Other than issues of the government of South Africa, this was the other issue that the entire South African society felt strongly about, and agreed to, whether they were black or white.

I believe it is this influence, of the Zimbabwean Diasporas, and the resulting refugee and refugee's problems, especially in the UK and

South Africa that Zimbabwe was dealt with this way. News organisations like etv, SABC, The Star, The Times, The Citizen drove the agenda on Zimbabwean issues' coverage in South Africa. There was a time when every news time or newspaper simply had news on Zimbabwe. I also want to believe it was the case in the UK, and other western countries, maybe due to Zimbabwe's Diasporas influence in these societies. This push from the outside was just as fierce as the push from the inside and resulted in the SADC, AU, and Mugabe himself kowtolling to this pressure, especially during the power sharing negotiations.

16. SADC and the AU should be given some credit, especially for convincing Mugabe to allow some level of political freedoms for the opposition party, in about 2 weeks before the March 2008 elections, and also for transparency throughout this polling period. The SADC guidelines of displaying election results on the notice board, at local ward level, once they had been counted, verified and collated made it difficult for ZANUPF and Mugabe to rig these elections. Before they were even through collating for the entire constituent, or province, or even the whole country, some people and organisations already had their predicted result. Even if ZEC were to cheat they could only have done that within acceptable ranges or figures, and it couldn't have influenced that much the final result. This is why ZANUPF's controlled police was angered and ended up arresting the MDC secretary general, Tendai Biti; and charging him with treason and inciting public disorder for predicting the result and confirming speculations that the MDC had won with the required percentage before the ZEC had made the final results available.

And even though stories were abound of vote rigging, especially during the time the ZEC sat on the results for over a month whilst the whole country waited anxiously and the whole world at large waited in dismay. At the end they had to accept the fact that they could not do much twisting of these results, because the gap was too big to cover up through rigging. There were stories of the ZEC having been held at hostage by the notorious CIO, that the CIO was managing the poll, telling the ZEC when and which ward result to release, the constituency or senate result. This was evident earlier on when the results from Harare were held back against the previous elections when results from Harare were always the first ones to come through. This time, even poll results from far-flung and inaccessible places like Binga were out before most of Harare's vote.

I remember when we were waiting for this result, at the company that I worked for and, we were also in the process of delivering some couple of trucks to a senior government minister. His guard, who was a CIO agent, whom we were dealing with, told us that Mugabe had been defeated by Tsvangirai and had accepted defeat but that the joint operations command (the Army, C.I.O, prison service and police alliance) had taken over, especially the CIO where he worked. That they had held Mugabe at hostage and told him that he couldn't resign and accept defeat. That he would either have to go for a run-off, or they would rig the entire election, out rightly. He even gave us the figure of 53per cent they were working on, by doing a complete rigging of the poll. This was also later-on supported by a well-known C.I.O agent at the company I worked for. The company I was working for is a government company and there are quite a number of C.I.O agents at this company, some of whom didn't even try to hide that. This particular agent was a leader of the war veterans and was said to be working at the president's desk.

Over the years I was at this company, a lot of government programmes, operations, and strategies were well known to us before they were even implemented. It was through this agent that we got to know of their impending implementation. But, despite all those possibilities of the rigging of the poll or stories of rigging that could have been pursued by the ZEC, and the CIO, it wasn't entirely workable to pursue them since the results had already been posted at ward-level. No matter what rigging they did, they simply had to accede that Tsvangirai had defeated Mugabe, but whether the final result was correct or not is another issue. The only regrettable speculation was that Tsvangirai could really have won the poll with the required percentage but that they had made it such that he would win not with the required percentage. If it is true, then whatever vote-rigging that was alleged to have been done at some army barracks, could have stayed Mugabe in power for some time, and defrauded Tsvangirai of a clear victory.

The new law had also made it possible for a runoff to follow. Though this was not a plus on Tsvangirai because if there was not such a change in the electoral laws, Tsvangirai should simply have won by using the previous electoral law, whatever the percentage? But, all this convinced a lot of doubters like the SADC, AU, Mbeki, and other ZANUPF apologists. Tsvangirai now had the popular support of the people. I would like to think Mbeki grudgingly accepted this. He must have regretted having to have twisted his friend Mugabe, to accept all those electoral laws that had resulted in this loss and embarrassment. A lot of people also now believed the often repeated MDC allegation that Mugabe always won in the previous elections through vote rigging. Most of the people concluded that Tsvangirai would win the runoff. There was no two ways about it if the poll was to be carried out in a free and fair way, because the gap of 4per cent was too big for Mugabe to cover up on, in a couple of months considering he had nothing new to offer to the electorate, but huge economic problems he didn't even have an idea on how to solve them.

17. Inversely, even though the SADC and AU brought Mugabe's popularity into scrutiny and, maybe due to some guilty conscience for the losses that Mugabe had incurred in this poll, they turned a blind eye after the March election on Mugabe as he militarised the country. Deep down the minds, of most of these African leaders, they wanted to protect Mugabe from international pressure and prosecution because most of these leaders are products, and or bye-products of the closely linked liberation movements that liberated the African continent. They were not so keen, especially Mbeki and SADC on a party that comes from the workers taking over. The worse thing was that the party was being supported by their former colonisers.

I think this protection, rather than being beneficial to Mugabe, in the long run, even increased pressure on him, on these African leaders also. The pressure even came from their own electorate, who were ashamed with their leaders, for trying to protect Mugabe who was bashing innocent citizens. It was also for the Zimbabwean issue that Mbeki was vilified throughout the world, just as he was especially vilified for the AIDS issue by the South Africans. This Zimbabwe issue was giving the entire Southern African region a bad face on the international front, especially considering that the football world cup was going to be held in 2010, in South Africa. Taking into consideration Stepp Blatter blatherings of a plan B to the world cup; that FIFA might take the world cup from South Africa, thus it must have pushed South Africa to solve Zimbabwe before this eventuality. They could deny it all they want to, but it was especially for the threat

133

of losing the world cup, that pushed South Africa, especially Mbeki and Motlanthe, into settling this issue as soon as was possible, especially during the last moments of the negotiations.

18. Another ordinary mistake but cardinal surviving tactic that Mugabe made was when he went on another mad drive to win the June 2008 elections. In the process he reckoned that he will either win it or disturb the entire process, thereby discrediting it altogether. He went for the jaguar, killing every dissent, maiming the undecided, militarise the country and close the country of, and stopped Tsvangirai from not even having a single campaign rally, and displaced the biggest part of Tsvangirai's voters. The idea could have been to win the election with whatever margin or to entirely disrupt it so that he could push for a negotiated political settlement, still with an upper hand. If Tsvangirai had allowed and accepted the challenge to compete in the runoff, with the 2.1 million votes that Mugabe later got, taking and leaving about half a million who would have abstained or spoilt the ballot, and another half a million who had been displaced, it could have taken care of over 3 million votes. Tsvangirai would have been beaten for polling the remainder 1.5 million or so.

One way or another, it seems, Mugabe and his team had set themselves for the bragging rights to bargain with more powers, but they would have liked to have won the election to put them in a position in which they could even have refused to enter into negotiations, altogether. The total madness that ensured during these elections made them totally discreditable. As a stroke of political brilliance, MDC struck a week before the elections, by withdrawing from the election. I remember how it stunned the whole country. They had the good evidence Mugabe had given them, especially the disbanding of Tsvangirai's only rally, and the subsequent beatings of observers from SADC by the police, army and C.I.O.

But like the political bulldozer he had been, Mugabe didn't give a fig that Tsvangirai had withdrawn, and continued with his one man "coconut" run off show. The whole world could only laugh it off. It was either re-elections, especially considering the impending sanctions and pressure from the UN, or the SADC and AU inspired negotiations. Like the good brothers to Mugabe, that African leaders have been, they protected Mugabe from the sanctions and they suggested UN supervised re-election route or pushed for a negotiated settlement. The negotiations ate into some of Mugabe's executive powers and cooled things for the time being in Zimbabwe, and pressure on Mugabe.

Unwinding this thread has been a long road and the thread is Mugabe. it has taken Zimbabwe all these years, all these pains, all these deaths, maiming, hopes, shattered dreams, to unwind this thread, to undo Mugabe. We are firmly set on another attempt to undo him again and what will come out of this attempt can only be seen down the line. Its success could only be with the departure of Mugabe from our political landscape, or maybe after another lifetime when we will have Mugabe confined in history book shelves. It has all been a process and that's the import of this piece of writing, which has been a look at these processes. It's not meant to be an "I-know-it-all or I-saw-it-all" indictment. I believe these are some of the processes that have brought Mugabe to this time and space, but the undoing process has not been completed. Mugabe is still the problem.

A Recipe on How to Create a Holocaust

W.H.O: There are over 778 people who have died of cholera and over 15 000 have been infected by the beginning of December 2008.

Tutu: Mugabe must be removed by force.

Bishop Ndungane: Mugabe is a modern day Hitler

Mugabe: There is no cholera in Zimbabwe . We have arrested it.

Ndlovu: It's all Britain's biological warfare against Zimbabwe.

Charamba: Mugabe was only joking, making a jest at the British.

Motlanthe : We will not ask Mugabe to step down

Botswana: Mugabe must step down

Tsvangirai: I wonder when I would ever get a passport to visit Zimbabwe

Zuma: Mugabe is no longer my comrade but I don't support the use of force against Mugabe

Zimbabwean diasporas: That two timing numbskull is trying to please both Mugabe and Welshman Ncube, for the sake of his little daughter, and also when he will be the president of South Africa next year

UK: We will wait until South Africa is off the presidency of the Security Council, in January 2009, for us to make another sanctions resolution on Zimbabwe.

Zimbabwean: Some more sanctions! Don't they see they are ineffective against Mugabe? They can only serve to hurt us some more, not Mugabe.

Russia: We will veto any resolution on Zimbabwe just to spite those bloody Americans and British.

China: We will do the same to protect our interest in Africa from those imperialists

Mid December 2008: Over 1100 have died of cholera

SADC: Silence

AU: Silence

UK: Waiting

UK/USA: We have withdrawn support for the power sharing deal.

Australia: We have done the same too, and we have included some more people on the targeted sanctions list. We have kicked, out of Australia, family members of ZANUPF leaders, especially students in Australian universities.

Tsvangirai: I will ask our national council to withdraw the MDC from the power sharing deal if Mugabe continues persecuting our supporters.

Mugabe: I will never ever go. Zimbabwe spirit mediums would never allow "Shoes" Bush to force me out.

Msika: Yezh prezhident, yezh your Excellency

Mugabe: Bush and that secretary of his think that Africans are idiots. They think we are little kids who cannot think for themselves.

Mbeki: I agree, totally

Motlanthe: To what? I didn't hear what you were talking of, but me too, I agree totally.

Kikitwe: I, too.

Mbeki: That's why we have decided as Africans to never allow Tsvangirai to be the president of Zimbabwe. He is controlled by Britain and the Americans. We have to believe in African renaissance whereby African problems must be solved by African leaders, and that's the reason why Patyana, in fact UNISA, have decided to create a leadership institute in my name; you know so that we will all learn how to solve our own problems.

Mugabe: Brilliant idea my friend! And talking of which, I would like to give some lecture, sometime in January when I take my annual leave, or even after I retire, in fact if I am ever going to retire at all.

Mbeki: That's the idea my friend, never ever worry for your place is there. You are top-drawer leader my friend. We are planning to invite other great leaders like Gaddafi, young Kabila, my good friend Al Bashir, Seso 'Ngueso, Kibaki and other many luminary African leaders.

Gono: We expect a GDP growth of 10 per cent for the coming year and contrary to the lies you have been hearing, we won't need food aid next year. I am going to print enough money for us to buy everything that we need for farming this year.

Mugabe: All Zimbabweans, you have heard it for yourself how prepared we are for anything and the kind of support we have all over the world. Don't worry about those Bush shits you are hearing these days. "There are just kicks from a dying horse". I know I will never be let down by Zimbabweans like what the Americans did to Bush, and the British did to that Blair toilet. You know what; the Blair toilet is now polluting some students at some university class in the middle of nowhere America, with his smell, of course.

ZANUPF supporters: Uluu lululu…. *Ululating to Mugabe at Manyika's funeral.*

Zimbabwean: Sick, sick, sick, I wonder when this talk, talk would ever end. Are they afraid of attacking militarily? Why can't they just bloody-hell bomb Mugabe out of our lives!

139

Zimbabwean: I am so hungry and thirsty, I can't talk anymore.

Zimbabwean: …

W.H.O: We are losing the battle with cholera due to the total collapse of the Zimbabwean economy and its health care system.

First Impressions: A Letter from South Africa

When I came into South Africa, by the beginning of April 2008, I could see some tell-tale signs; that the country was firmly on the downward trend. I kept wondering, for some time and, having this sense that South Africa could be going down the Zimbabwean way, that is, towards a failed state. If you listen to the political discourse coming from the media, if you listen to the South African politicians, you can't help having this foreboding feeling that things are not going the right way. In the newspapers, you hear of the politicians talking about muzzling the media, tempering with the constitution, courts and judges, tempering with the day to day running and functioning of private institutions, government departments, democracy institutions and even the local and provincial governments. This being done to protect some select leaders (the sacred cows of the ANC) from being criticised and prosecuted (there is a corruption and bribery case against the ANC president, Jacob Zuma).

You get sick every day listening to this and that judge (government apologist, Judge Hlope), this and that politician (Julius Malema of the ANC youth league), this and that trade unionist (Zwelinzima Vavi of COSATU(Confederation of South African Trade Unions) all jostling to destroy the pillars of democracy, to suite their own entrenched needs. One of the politicians (Blade Nzimande of the South African Communist Party) went to the extent of referring to the constitutional court as a "kangaroo court." A term, some years ago, that was used to refer to the Zimbabwe's supreme and constitutional court by the ZANUPF political machinery before ZANUPF destroyed its independence by hounding out its fine judges like Gubbay, Blackie and Smith. Now it is filled up with ZANUPF apologists.

You also hear of these ANC tripartite politicians spiting at the people who voted them; and the nation at large, with their questionable support of Zuma, whether guilty or not. They go to the extent of saying that they would kill for Zuma (the "we will kill for Zuma" speeches) if he is found guilty of the above referred to charges. Some are even advocating for the scrapping of the case at the courts; saying that it would disrupt government and the country by creating a power vacuum, if Zuma is still under prosecution and is eventually prosecuted when he will be the country's president. They are perpetuating this belief that the incumbent, or their chosen politician, has to be protected from the rule of law, that without him; there seem to be no other alternative. Mugabe did the same in Zimbabwe and up until now there is no real successor to him in the ZANUPF because of this entrenched belief that no one else is better.

From all this discourse, you end up getting the feeling that maybe Zuma is the only person in the whole of South Africa who is qualified to lead the nation. What qualities does he have? This Zuma is the same person who was tried for allegedly raping an HIV positive relative, a couple or so years ago, but was later acquitted after proving that it was consensual sex. Do you know what he said when he was asked whether he wasn't afraid he had caught the virus? He said he wasn't afraid because just after having sex with this woman, he had bathed himself in water and oiled himself with baby oil. I suppose, for once in their often acrimonious relationship, Mbeki couldn't help but admire his protégé.

Mbeki himself had taken years and years of refusal and denial, only to end up grudgingly admitting and accepting the existence of HIV. Even after admitting to this, he still believed the crazy beliefs of his health minister (Manto Msimang-Shabalala); that traditional medicines have a better headway than western medicines (anti-retroviral drugs) in the treatment of this disease. Today there is general acceptance that over 350 000 people who died, in all the time it took them to eventually roll out the anti-retroviral drugs, shouldn't have died had they done that earlier. I don't know whether this would qualify for a crime against humanity?

The other worrying thing in South Africa is the level of violence across the society. It is so tangible. South Africa is rated as the third most violent country in the world. Inside every 2 days there are over 80 killings committed. The violence has spawned into schools where inside every two weeks there is a recorded violence and killing case. It is estimated that last year there were over 15 000 violent killings in South Africa. This number is the same number of people who were also killed in the roads, due to negligence and reckless driving. Contrast this with just about 150 or so people who die from the roads in Australia, I think you understand what I am alluding to. Street and road races are an everyday thing in South Africa's roads.

South Africa is, unfortunately, a wacky society; a demented society held together by thin glue. South Africa's economy is slowing down under an impending recession, interest rate hikes and inflation. It's getting worse every day. There are now predicting a growth rate of

143

about 3per cent rather than the 5per cent they had predicted in the first place. Everywhere you go in South Africa; it is this talk of this doom. The other day I was reading some articles in the magazines, on how many South Africans were considering leaving South Africa. Across all the races, it was an average of 30-50per cent. In the articles, over 20per cent of South Africa's white population had left South Africa after independence, about 45 000-70 000 former white South Africans were now said to be staying in New Zealand alone, and over 50 000 are in and around Perth Australia alone, not to talk of the million or so in the UK. Both educated black and white South Africans are making it first choice to look for employment outside of South Africa. They are both sick of the ANC leadership and mismanagement of the economy and, skills shortage is the order of the day in South Africa.

I keep wondering whether this is another sinking titanic in the make- according to the prophetic words of Levy Mwanawasa- who had predicted the demise of Zimbabwe and likened it to the sinking of the titanic.

The other cancer that is eating into South Africa is corruption. It has pervaded every level of the society. In South Africa you can hear, in the press, of people struggling to get their identity papers because their papers had been collected by someone else or because their names have been used up by other people with the same details. That the computers won't process another set of papers. Some women are married off to people they don't even know of and it's difficult for them to annul these marriages.

The home affairs department is one of the most corrupt departments in South Africa. The police and immigration department are a close behind in terms of corruption. Now, some people can't get employment, some can't open bank accounts and access credit facilities, some can't continue with their education, some have been arrested for crimes they never committed, or credits or debts their unknown spouses incurred in their names.

You can stay in South Africa, even for a lifetime without papers; even a foreigner can do that without getting deported. As long as you have the monies to bribe the police and immigrations officials, you can stay there permanently. You can even cross, re-cross, several times the Beitbridge border post, through immigration and customs without papers.

There Is No Xenophobia in South Africa

News of foreigners in South Africa being killed by the South Africans, i.e., black South Africans killing black Africans, which some writer referred to as Negrophobia for better terminology, started filtering through to Zimbabwe where I had returned to on 11 May 2008 to process my travel documents. They were especially killing the Zimbabweans, Zambians, Malawians, Mozambicans, Somalis and Nigerians, whom they accused of among others; theft, corruption, stealing their jobs, the economic downturn, stealing their wives, children…, even at that, allegations which up until now haven't been proven.

I have always known, in fact a lot of Africans know that South Africans are xenophobic, rabidly so. Most of the South Africans believe that they inhabit their own Africa, even during liberation wars that were the feelings within the African body politic and writing at that time; a sort of Diasporas Africa and that the rest of the continent is all about wars, savagery, backwardness, smelling to quote some South Africans' beliefs. But these South Africans suffer total amnesia to the fact that during apartheid South Africa, they bunked out of their country and were treated well by these same nationalities they were now killing. A very good example is Mbeki himself who stayed in Zimbabwe. I remember there was a South African student at my A-level school, Marist Nyanga high school, in 1992-1993.

In May 2008, we also read in the newspapers, of foreigners being chased out of the township suburbs, of foreigners being told to "go back" to their countries, of foreigners being raped, killed, maimed, and burned alive. Even the black South Africans of foreign origins were also killed. You only had to know the name of an elbow in Zulu for you to be spared of this.

It took the South African (ANC leadership rather than the government of Mbeki) 3 weeks to decide to deploy the soldiers into the streets to quell this violence, which had left 63 people dead and hundreds of thousands homeless. The army is now off the streets, but only a week ago, I read in the newspapers of a Ugandan national being killed in xenophobic anger after returning back to his township home, thinking that this negrophobia anger had abetted. You read in the newspapers of the government forcing these victims of xenophobia to be repatriated into their communities or face deportations, even so when the government knows that it is not safe in those townships. That, they would be killed if they return back into those communities, and to top it all, there is naked dislike and harassment of foreigners by the government itself, especially Zimbabweans. The police and home affairs officials are now more arrogant than their apartheid counterparts; are increasingly brutalizing the vulnerable with impunity, especially foreigners.

A couple of days ago (on 26 July 2008) my older brother, his wife and their friends were having a private party in Hillbrow, a Johannesburg eastern suburb predominantly occupied by foreigners when the police abruptly disrupted their party, and arrested everyone at that bar (over 50 people) for drinking in a public place when they were rightly drinking in a bar, which doesn't in any way, constitute public drinking for that matter. The crux of the matter was that they had

147

been arrested because they were Zimbabweans, and that being Zimbabweans that they were, and that most of their fellow nationals having had refused to be repatriated or deported in the earlier case of xenophobia violence victims, so they were now being punished for the sins of the other group.

They had to bribe these police officers in order to be released out of police custody. One can't help asking what wrong Zimbabweans did to deserve this inhuman treatment. There is no safe place for Zimbabweans other than in Limpopo River, which is infested with crocodiles because on both sides of the Limpopo River they are being killed with reckless abandon. Nobody seems to care in South Africa, not even the president himself.

Mbeki could go to the extent of refusing to recognise that South Africans were xenophobic, on the memorial day of the victims. But the murder of 31 Somalis in the Cape, in September 2006, and how the whole thing was bungled by the officials set precedent to this xenophobia. Yet Mbeki out rightly rejected this notion again, and thus he rejected it for his people. He assigned this scourge, according to him, to a third force or a few criminals (counter revolutionary forces) who were doing this to destabilise and blacken their country. Criminals to talk of which, some of whom have been apprehended, but none has been tried or convicted. This outstanding failure by the police to bring people to book, this official lethargy demonstrates the state's own prejudices and xenophobia against immigrants. Suppose those 31 were British nationals, were they going to be that unconcerned and lethargic in dealing with the issue?

This denial of Mbeki did not surprise a lot of people, because over the years, a lot of people have come to know that Mbeki believes his people do not think for themselves. That he has to think for them. So like on the AIDS issue, the Zimbabwean political crises' issue, so also now on this xenophobia issue. There is no AIDS issue to talk of, no Zimbabwean issue, and no xenophobia issue to talk of. Case dismissed, guilty dispatched…

But an even look across the tribes or language groups in South Africa, it is so clear that they are intolerant of each other. So that xenophobia, it seems, has to do with South Africa's inability to deal with the race issue constructively. Thabo Mbeki's inability to deal with this, in actual fact, his inability to deal with Mugabe is because of his inability to deal with the inner race issues, or inner Zimbabwe, and conversely, his inner Africa.

Zulus don't like the Xhosas, Sothos don't like the Tswanas, Swazis don't like the Pedis and the Pedis don't like Vendas, Ndebeles don't like Tsongas, English don't like Afrikaans, Chinese against Indians, whites against blacks, blacks against fellow blacks, blacks against Chinese South Africans for being included in the disadvantaged races in BEE (black economic empowerment) deals, but all this is ignored. So that one would get the feeling that it's all about the scramble of the economic pie, but deep down, it's a deeply rooted feeling of distrust, of the next person or race or language. During South Africa's apartheid it was Mongosuthu's Zulus against Mandela's Xhosas, and now it is Zuma's Zulus against Mbeki's Xhosas. But what sells is black against white, with blacks as victims. This creates a lot of noise in South Africa.

This one sided portrayal of victimisation perpetuates and feeds into the "woundedness" of the black people and breeds a sick sense of entitlement, often lacking in migrants and refugees. It breeds an ethos

149

in the victims that they can never be wrong, and that they are owed a livelihood. It denies the fact that the oppressed can be so racistic and discriminatory. These attacks on immigrants by the blacks attest to that. Racism flourish in context where it has been internalised to such an extent that the victims begin to miss it- to want it- when it begins to disappear and so they will invoke it. When migrants come and make it out of their own will and hard work. It challenges this victim status quo and rankles and these migrants become the scourge of South Africans' angers. So that these tribes and language groups would sometimes forget it's all about tribal distrust and intolerance, between the tribes, and collectively rent their anger and frustrations on the unsuspecting foreigners who are an easier scapegoat for all these tribal or racial bile.

South Africa is unfortunately a wacky society. It is rated as the third most violent country in the world. Inside every 2 days there are over 80 killings committed, and the violence has even spanned into schools where inside every 2 weeks there is a recorded violence or killing case. It is also estimated that in 2008 alone they were over 15000 violence killings that occurred in South Africa. Mbeki would want us to believe that just these few individuals were the prime cause of this upheaval. Just like in Nazi Germany, here are whole societies like Primrose, Alexandria, and Tembisa who upraised against foreigners. And it spread throughout the whole country.

In his book on Rwanda, "When victims become killers", Mahmoud Mamdani warns that when the simple prejudices becomes transmogrified into hate crimes and later ethnic conflicts, the consequences are difficult to reverse. Think of Rwanda, Burundi, DRC, and Bosnia and, Israel is doing to the Palestinians what the Nazi Germans did to them, over 50 years ago.

150

Someday I took a taxi from Malvern, an inner city middle lower class suburb of east Johannesburg. I was sited besides a young lady and when my phone rang, I answered my brother in my mother tongue, Shona. Everyone in that taxi turned around to stare at me, and afterwards I could hear some people conversing in Xhosa, and Zulu derogatory things about Makwerekwere (dirty scavengers), as Zimbabweans are known here. When someone disembarked from the taxi, that girl who had been sited besides me moved to occupy the vacated seat. I could only behave as if I hadn't heard anything or seen what that girl had done. Everywhere you go you can hear South Africans saying some bad things about foreigners.

I remember reading an article in Time Magazine, in the mid-1990s entitled, Echoes of the holocaust, on the Nazi war. The magazine was accusing Switzerland for its silence on the war atrocities and non-involvement in the allies' cause, and of its help of the Nazi war machine. The article also accused Swiss banks for holding on to money of holocaust victims and the article concluded that it was the Swiss' right to have had trade with Nazi Germany but had issues with its moral bankruptcy for allowing this, and to be a part of the Axis. It concluded that the Swiss should, at least, return the monies looted from the Jews and to also apologise for its involvement.

South Africans and Mbeki could be doing the same thing to Zimbabweans, by turning a blind eye on the persecuted in Zimbabwe and in South Africa, in order to preserve trade and friendship with Mugabe. Mbeki and the leadership in South Africa should be helping the blacks in South Africa to deal with their collective woundedness.

Exile

We are like a migrant blackbird. We are an alien traveller looking for grains, sun and the sand of rivers. Like the blackbird, we complain about the sad shadows; wind, rain, mountains, rivers, insecure nights, even of our own shouts. We are always wishing we had the power to rest from all that. Fasting for weeks on end in our journeys, fasting to purify the mind, of the ugliness we have left behind, to clean the wells of old foggy minds. We have black hair; it is a river, the Limpopo River for it reaches some places far off. The northern border of South Africa is an old scar that will not heal until there are no more deaths there. As long as there are deaths, it will always be a sore spot.

There are still deaths from suffocating trailer trucks, car engines, car trunks, dying from hot boxcars with no air to breathe, from running across the freeways, dying from swimming across the Limpopo River, dying from crossing into unhospitable and inhospitable places along the border area. There are deaths from heat strokes, kidney failures, dying in the hope of finding work. We will die anyway, in Limpopo River, trying to dodge the marauding crocs. We will die in the dense forests dodging searing bullets from vigilant justice, police and army. We will die trying to dodge the marauding wild animals, perhaps writhing and smarting in a glinting coil of barbed wire, perhaps sprawling under the merciless glare of the afternoon sun. There are pregnant women dying, crossing Limpopo to join their men folk; dying in the hope of re-uniting the family. There are deaths of children accompanying these women, too.

Back home, in Zimbabwe, we had to leave home afraid of dying. We fled Zimbabwe because life was too harsh and oppressive. They were no individual freedoms anymore. Our freedoms were trampled upon. We were butchered, we were killed, and we were maimed by the politicos. Some of us couldn't find food in the shops, tired of endless queues to secure basic commodities. Some of us were farmers whom cheap agribusiness imports drove us quickly of the lands, some of us had our land taken forcefully by the government. Some of us our wages had been lowered due to increased presence of machinery, and the meltdown of the economy and industry, such that we had ended up specialising in skills so unexceptionally, so insignificant, and became virtually unskilled.

For some time we struggled to make ends meet with all this until we couldn't take care of our families on our own, so we asked our families to join us in those workplaces in Zimbabwe. Our children and spouses were simply compelled to join us to help us. They entered this relentless race against death. We all persevered until we couldn't sustain ourselves anymore in our country, so we left Zimbabwe for South Africa. We had no other choice. We came into South Africa because we believed they would understand us, and that had they been the ones they would have done the same thing for their families.

In South Africa we work jobs that nobody else wants, so if we leave as they are saying we should return back to Zimbabwe, who would do those jobs? There is always a war to rid us out of South Africa. This war is simply fought against those who plant and harvest crops, those who work at Burger king and MacDonald's, clean houses and lawns and gardens, those who pack meat at the meat factories, at the foundry man, at women who man garment factories, at men polishing windshields and shoes at corner streets, at women selling treats, men bagging trash, fixing roofs, painting walls, women doing shopping, caring for children, men laying foundations to factories and new towers.

The only way to go now; we should be given full rights as immigrants so that we won't be exploited. We should have the right to dream. We should have an obligation to dream. We can't forever pick fruit and beans and pull potatoes. After all South Africa would be nothing without our sacrifices, so we deserve to dream. What kind of a land that would say "come and work but don't develop any ambitions, don't dream"?

But we really have no right to anything in South Africa, yet we work our asses, building careers and lives. We have to content everyday with the police. If we lose our identity papers in South Africa, it would be like we have forgotten our names to the South African police. We are called a threat, a problem, and a menace to the peace and safety of the towns, cities, and the country. The media, schools, churches and government supply endless instances of our supposed criminality, seeds meant to sow hate and distrust in citizen people's hearts. And the citizens would fear us, fearing that we would take their jobs, sell drugs, bomb ATMs, mug them, vandalise or loiter and litter their streets, steal their wives, and endless other absurd accusations.

We are paid very low wages but we still take the jobs that citizen people refuse to take because if we are to complain to the bosses about these low wages and conditions, we instantly will be fired from our jobs. The bosses would call the police, telling them we were

154

illegal. They would just fire us, anyway. Even after working our lives to the grind. We can't even dream of putting our case across to the citizens because they want us out. The citizens haul racial insults at us, at our appearances, our customs, our languages, our intellect, even the sizes of our families. They release so much hatred and violence at us, so much irrationality. After they have released their frustrations and hate, they seem briefly satisfied. Their bosses would be happy to see them return back to work with renewed strength and newer disposition. They even go to the streets demanding that the government act immediately to expel us out of their country. Naturally they can always count on one or two bigoted lawmakers and media bites to draft a bill that brands us as criminals.

We are devoured by the twin beasts, credit and debt, carrying six figures mortgages. We are abused by a system of mass exploitation.

And if we can't speak the local languages then we will be in a lot of hot soup. We live in fear every working moment, and after work, our hearts almost come out of our mouths, our legs running. We are tired of running away from the police as we make it to our homes, our jails, our temples. Home is where we breathe and take stock and regroup for the morrow day. We can't really loiter outside. We don't stand in full view of the police or immigration who always threatens to catch us and deport us back to Zimbabwe.

Our children live in a void of despair and solitude until the streets finally lure them away from us with the false promises of adventure and meaning. In the streets our children are fed with draft beers instead of milk, raped by landlords to gain good stead, are refused schooling, run errancy as call girls, and are given to marriages to foreigners, suffer from sexually transmitted diseases and imprisonment. There is day to day increase of young beggars in the streets, illiterate children, and unemployable young and middle aged people. We don't have anywhere to go.

We were born alien in our countries so we don't really belong anywhere but in our tiny shelters where we huddle together. Seeing beyond this present becomes futile. Our ideas are failing us in this chaos. Toiling, weeping and starving, hurling and tossing the leaden embers of misery into the leaping fires of hope. Hunger, poverty, diseases, death redoubled our desire to settle in South Africa, redefining South Africa in our hearts, turning it into a seductive myth, a force of nature, a land of unique possibilities for us.

Malemania

What is the meaning of this word, Malemania? Malema; there is a certain Julius Malema in South Africa who was the president of the ANC youth league. From this surname, was coined the word, Malemania. This explanation would give some idea as to how this character behaves or carries out his business. Like a maniac. When he was elected the president of the youths in 2007, in Bloemfontein, the youths had to fight knife battles during their elections. Afterwards they went on binge beer drinking madness in which they had photos taken whilst naked. This heralded the dawn of the Malemania time in South Africa. Next stop was at the now politically revered Polokwane ANC conference, the city formerly known as Petersburg. Here the youths pushed for the ouster of Mbeki from the president of the ANC, by backing Zuma. They did this with the help of CASATU and the Communist Party; with of course help from former ANC youth leaders who were now in the ANC like Fikile Mbalula and Nath Mtetwa. The two are now ministers in the Zuma government.

And thus, at Polokwane, Zuma was able to dethrone Mbeki. And then it continued with the speeches "we will kill for Zuma", and he upped Blade Nzimande's description of the judiciary as the "kangaroo courts", or even upped Gwede Mantashe's description of courts as "counter revolutionary forces." Jacob Zuma's corruption trials were one of the biggest problems to Malema's learning and development. His calls for "we will kill for Zuma" were licensed by

157

the elders. The fact that the trial had to be dropped without being pursued to conclusion in a court of law was a mistake. In 2009, the National Prosecution Authority (NPA) had to drop the charges after Max Hulley (Zuma's lawyer) mysterious came into possession of leaked tapes, with evidence of political meddling, against Zuma. It had conversations between Bulelani Ngcuka (NPA boss), and Leonard McCarthy (Scorpions boss, the crimes investigations part of the police) who were alleged to be heard discussing the timing of Zuma's charges to give an advantage to his rival, Mbeki. Malema was backed to the hilt by the ANC leadership that kept quiet and never rebuked this fellow with his "we will kill for Zuma" speeches.

He went on the overdrive by even mocking the ANC deputy president, the level headed Kgalema Motlanthe, who he said was behaving reverently towards him, especially his level headed take at the judiciary, courts and Malema issues. He said Motlanthe was being politically correct every time. The ANC, particularly Zuma didn't bring this person to book, and thus they allowed this Malemania disease to proliferate. Then he went for the top gun of South Africa's government, Mbeki, whom he lambasted at every turn, going to the extent of driving and pushing for his ouster as the country's president.

After successfully doing that the fellow couldn't help preening about that and boasting that it was his, and his alone influence, that had caused the recall of Mbeki from government by the ANC. After this he went for the opposition party leaders like Helen Zille referring to her as some sort of a white Michael Jackson, who was feigning to be black when deep down she was white, racist, and an Afrikaner. Saying that Zille doesn't want the black man to be rulers and that she was always critical of the ANC policies, that she was an unconstructed racist, saying that she had her own male concubines, thus referring to the fact that the Zille Western Cape government had mostly, if not all, male MECs. He even brazenly referred to her as a prostitute, who had slept with every of her MECs. Still on these sick sexist beliefs of his, he later lambasted that relative of Zuma who once accused Zuma of raping her, saying that this woman had enjoyed the sex? According to him, any woman who has been raped wouldn't wait for breakfast the morrow morning and ask for bus fares later.

Then he went for the Shilowa and Lekoto arrangement (COPE, i.e., Congress of People) and these two leaders, saying that they were just power hungry individuals who would want to try to hold on to power if they were elected. That COPE is a black DA party (Helen Zille's party is the D.A, i.e., Democratic Alliance), that they wanted to perpetuate white supremacist policies and leadership. Then he went for Mongosuthu Buthelezi (IFP, i.e. Inkhata Freedom Party) leader, saying that he was a dictator. That he was like Mugabe, whom surprisingly, he is now friends with after being smothered by that clever dictator, when he visited Mugabe at his den Zimbabwe. After that he made a go at the education minister then, Naledi Pandor, saying that Pandor should use her foreign accent to help address problems students were facing at universities and schools.

It is wrong to assume, so far, that Malemania is only Malema's phenomena. It is bigger than Malema. Zuma and the whole ANC leadership are as much Malemania as Malema is. Look at how appointments for public service jobs are carried out, then you will realise it's deeper than Malema himself. Zuma had to piss on the process of judiciary succession that required sensitive management by disregarding it altogether, and picked up a judge of his own choice. Judge Moseneke who had been the deputy to Pius Langa had the first

159

right to be picked to succeed Langa but was overlooked for Mogoeng Mogoeng, who was a junior to Moseneke. There is huge love lost between Zuma and Moseneke which goes back to during the liberation fight. Inversely, the problems of all these administrative bungling, on future South Africans, is now being felt with Malema. Future South Africans are being habituated to public culture fractions in the extreme.

All these throw a light on the bigger issue, the relationship between the old and young, that is; there is no balancing adult authority such that the young leaders are likely to descent into chaos and murderous anarchy, without this adult authority which is lacking in South Africa. Malema now is the most ridiculed person in South Africa today, and a look in any newspaper or a listen at the electronic Medias, would definitely have some mention of this character, Malema. Those who defend him say that those who criticise him do not know his real job. They say his job is that of an activist, or that of a revolutionary. That Malema should be like Mandela when Mandela was the youth league leader himself. Mandela was said to have pushed for the ouster of a former ANC president, Desmond Dube, when he was the youth league leader.

Lately, Malema is now facing disciplinary charges for "bringing the ANC into disrepute and sowing divisions within the ANC ranks." He was also accused for calling for the land reform in the form of Zimbabwe's, the removal of Ian Khama from the presidency of Botswana, saying Khama is a dictator. But, it seems, Zuma, with both his trials and the government appointments, is always bringing the party and country into disrepute but nobody has been able to bring him to book. Malema wouldn't see any difference to what he was being accused of.

But, all that is happening to Malema now is due to lack of adult balancing and grooming leadership. I will be the first to refract from saying everything that Malema has been doing is wrong, no. it is always good for young people, like Malema, to test social limits but there is always need of adult balancing authority to provide ethical, moral, legal, intellectual, spiritual, political and even corrective limits. Without which the energies of young people usually would transform into revolt and anarchy. This elderly guidance should not be of force(like what the ANC and Zuma's authority has become, by taking Malema through disciplinary without trying to teach him on the right way of doing things.) It should be of care, intelligence, principle, civility and dignity. Malema is simply a young boy crying out for help, for guidance which he singularly lacked from young age. He didn't grow up with his father, so he is crying for a fatherly figure and guidance.

I want to think that since no one was good enough to fill that void in Malema, in the ANC, he is looking across the northern border, and that's why he has been developing a closer relationship with the ZANUPF party, and especially Mugabe. Mugabe, in his eyes, must be filling this void of a fatherly figure. Inversely it's what Mugabe is crying out for, too. For young people who would recognise him as a fatherly figure. But deeper down, with Mugabe, it is always about securing his future (posterity). Mugabe will simply use this character Malema like he has used some earlier models of this Malemania disease in Zimbabwe to create political mileage. The problem will be he will just be urged on by Mugabe and the ZANUPF and exposed to no significant sense of limitation, parameters, and boundaries like what the ANC was doing to him.

Is Mugabe supporting Malema because he has realised the ANC doesn't support him anymore?

Now that the ANC leaders are victims to Malema, these seniors want to discipline their Mary Shelley's Frankenstein invention. The ANC later found Malema guilty of the charges of bringing the ANC into disrepute. They subsequently suspended him, and later, expelled him from the ANC after his appeal against suspension was overturned. Lately, he has been facing money laundering charges. It might be a little too late now. Malema is now a good example of West African child soldiers. So it seems, this Malemania disease, is not really a new disease, but simply a new strain of an old disease.

A look across the border, this Malemania disease was perfected by Jonathan Moyo and to a lesser extent by Border Gezi, Elliot Manyika, and now Savious Kasukuwere, but it was Moyo who perpetuated this disease in Zimbabwe. He would criticize everyone, including senior ZANUPF leaders, everyone except for Mugabe. In Zimbabwe this disease ended up in the misguided creation of a militant youth in the form of ZANUPF youths. And these ZANUPF green bombers (the militant Border Gezi trainees) terrorised innocent people in Zimbabwe, during the election period from 2002 up to now. The same militancy had, of course, started with the war veterans in the 2000 referendum, the farm invasions and the 2000 elections. This disease is prevalent all over the continent. It is the source of most of the wars in Africa at the present moment. Names like Laurent Kabila, Joseph Kabila, Laurent Nkunda, Jonas Savimbi, Armando Ferreira, John Garang, and the list is endless, have something to do with this disease, Malemania. The galling thing is to realise that there don't seem to be any cure for this disease on the continent.

162

Doing South Africa

Former Nigerian president, Olusegun Obasanjo who led the Africa alliance observer's mission in KZN (KwaZulu Natal) province in the last general elections, in 2009, declared the election as free and fair. He also gave sage wisdom to president Zuma, saying that he was now the president of the whole country, that he was like rain, and like rain which doesn't choose which fields to rain in, that he should rain in every field in the country, whether sinners, whether saints. I will add, whether White, Coloured, Asian, or Black. The sad thing to draw from this sage advice is that African countries always learn about this at the last moment when things cannot be reversed anymore. Most, If not all, African countries have made this same mistake, one after another. It is painful and galling to notice that the last hope of Africa (South Africa) seems to be on the same track.

I have been able to stay for over two years in South Africa. It has afforded me the opportunity to observe South Africa so that whatever I will articulate in this essay is not necessarily armchair understanding of the issues. I want to think that South Africa's biggest problem, like all the other African countries before it, is its failure to develop an alternative opposition party for the electorate to vote for. In the election of 2009, ANC still got over 60per cent of the vote, and all the other parties had to share the less than 40per cent of vote, with the DA (Democratic Alliance) getting a significant 24per cent of the vote. The DA is a vibrant opposition party and it could be an alternative for the electorate, barring one huge problem, that is, it is still viewed as a white supremacist party by the majority blacks. The majority blacks don't simply trust it. At one time there was a great vibe when COPE (Congress of People) came before the elections but it only garnered 8per cent of the vote, despite the fact that it had former ANC heavyweights like Lekota and Shilowa. It is now dying the same death of the UDM, ID, IFP parties, with infighting over positions being the biggest problem of its death. The sad reality is there is no party that can be able to unseat the ANC in the coming 2-3 election periods. That's the biggest threat to South Africa's young democracy, to have the ANC ruling the country for another 10 years, especially looking at what it is doing right now.

This lack of an alternative opposition party, this lack of an opposition (credible party) has resulted in the ANC parliamentarians' rubber stamping the ANC policies without much analysis or criticisms in the parliament. Ultimately, poor policies or decisions from the party have been implemented. Ralph Heintzman, a distinguished Canadian writer and academic said one of the most important feature of the parliament, is its deep symbolic value as the citadel of dialogue and civilised debate, noting. "The daily confrontation and "loyal' opposition in the House of commons (the parliament) symbolises the inner dialogue, the continual sequence of question and answer, which distinguishes the truly civilised mind and is reflected in the social and public life of a civil community. Just like a genuinely sound mind does not suppress either of its two fundamental impulses but instead listens to both, and tries unceasingly to achieve a synthesis in which their opposition will be reconciled, so too, the good society recognises the opposing tendencies are not each other's enemies but each other's partners instead, and their indispensable component. They are linked in an educational contract which is at once the condition and sign of civilisation." This is what is lacking in South

Africa's young democracy. A credible parliament and a credible opposition party such that South Africa's parliament doesn't provide a platform and forum in which points of view can be argued and in which through constant battle of opposing views and ideas, they could hope to find the truth. A sound parliament would be the source of effective social affiliation, can yield a sense of security, and an index of the citizen's happiness. By definition a majority of anything is not everything.

There is the school of analysts who believe that the breakup of the tripartite ruling alliance will usher such a credible opposition party. I believe it's not likely to happen very soon, and also the break up wouldn't offer much now. The other partners in the alliance (COSATU and the Communist Party) don't garner a lot of votes, even now on their own. It's the ANC that's the draw card in this tripartite arrangement. It's not very likely the other two members of this alliance will willingly leave this arrangement. They know they will die the same death as the IFP, ID, and UDM etc. The ANC will squeeze them out. COSATU (Confederation of South African Trade Unions) has future potential, though, but it would take some time for its potentiality to be realised. It would have to depend on the workers. When the work force rise up against the ANC government, not their employers like what has been happening, that's when CASATU could be relevant. That's the only viable realignment of South Africa's politics that I see but it needs time, which might not be there. Maybe when this happens the mismanagement of the economy will be irreversible.

Our problem, us the African electorate and I have noted it in another essay, "The Blame Game", is our post-independence acquiescing to our leaders. Judith Todd in her memoir, "Through the Darkness" also notes this and blames it for the destruction of democracy and countries in Africa. She reminds us of how the whole of Zimbabwe acquiesced to Mugabe's alienation politics and killings of the Ndebele people, which even the whole world was aware of but also kept a blind eye on. This resulted in over 20 000 deaths in the Matebeleland regions. This is what the black South Africans(mostly) is doing to the ANC, because, to them, it liberated them and also, the majority South Africans believes the ANC should be given time to make mistakes and learn from them. This is understandable but the problem is that it seems not to be learning anything from its mistakes, in fact the ANC don't feel they have to learn anything. The ANC knows that without a credible opposition party their power base will always be secure so they could as well mess things knowing that they are unaccountable.

This leads me to the next issue, which is of corruption. I have witnessed corruption happening in Zimbabwe and bringing Zimbabwe to its knees. I have come to realise that it's even a lot worse in South Africa. I can talk of B.E.E. (Black Economic Empowerment) deals, the minister's abuse of public funds, municipalities mismanagement by local authorities, and the mismanagement of government institutions due to political meddling. The public protector, The Land Bank, The Independent Complains Directorate, the SABC, Telkom, Eskom… and the list is endless. I want to start with electricity mismanagement.

Eskom; which produces electricity, sells it to City Power, and City Power sells it to the local municipalities, and these would sell it to the final consumers. All along this long supply chain there is massive corruption and by the time it filters to the final consumer, it will be so expensive. This is the true story I was told by a distant relative

166

who owns a property, a residential property in Ekurhuleni, South Africa. For the past two years she has accumulated a bill of about 50 000 Rands, that's around 7 000 dollars. The City Council started disconnecting electricity. No matter how much she had tried to pay up, she couldn't keep abreast with the charges because they were simply too exorbitant. They definitely had to accumulate to those amounts. She didn't have the money to pay up the credit. They came to plug out electricity, she later went to their offices.

The credit controller she talked to said she could either pay 10per cent, which is 5 000 Rands, for them to reconnect her or she could pay about 3 000 plus 100 Rands drink money. She took this alternative and parted away with 3 100 Rands rather than 5 000 Rands. The next month she paid 2 000 Rands, which she could afford that month and went to see that credit controller before they had disconnected the electricity. She showed him the slip of the 2 000 Rands that she had paid but the credit controller was concerned that the amount paid was little. She told him that's all that she could afford that month. He asked for his drink money and she gave him 100 Rands, and then he told her she had to wait for those who did the disconnections. He told her the time they were doing the disconnections in her area. She waited for them that day and talked to them, and they asked for the drink money. They were the two of them so she parted away with 200 Rands but she had electricity for the whole of that month.

Next month, she didn't even bother to pay anything. She waited for those who disconnected electricity and bribed them and this continued for some months. I haven't been in touch with her to check whether she is still doing that, but I suppose she still owns the property. Those guys who did disconnections would knock at the gates until she gets out for their bribe monies, in fact, they wouldn't disconnect, unless of course, she didn't pay any drink money.

She was also approached by the guy who did the recording of electricity metres. He told her that the charge of electricity was too high, and that he could sort the metre so that it could move slowly, at a snail's pace. At first she was incredulous about it all but he showed her the recordings and bills of those he had sorted their metres, and the very small charges they were now paying. He told her he had sorted a lot of metres in her area so she asked him to temper with hers. He did that and, she was accumulating very little in charges afterwards. It wasn't because the metre was dysfunctional but because the electricity charges were just too expensive.

Another way in which Eskom is losing revenue is through illegal connections to the national grid. The bulk of the slum towns and cities are illegally connected. The people don't pay Eskom. Considering that these slum cities and towns constitute a huge portion of South Africa's urban areas, there is definitely a huge loss of revenue through these illegal connections. Thinking of all that makes me realise the kind of revenue Eskom and the local municipalities are losing through that and, the corruption at all these levels. This will eventually bring down Eskom and the local municipalities.

Corruption in South Africa is happening in every municipality, every company, every non-governmental organisation, and every government department. It isn't happening only at the top echelons of South Africa's leadership, but right down to the street Joes.

Another ugly face of corruption is through the BEE (Black Economic Empowerment) deals, which is simply, "black elite enrichment". Patrice Motsepe has acquired more wealth through empowerment than did say (Pick n Pays) Raymond Ackerman, in half a century through hard work. Now the Motsepes are one of the wealthiest families in South Africa. There was also a huge controversy when Nelson Mandela's grandson and Jacob Zuma's nephew got control of a controversial mine (Aurora mine) in a deal in excess of 9 billion Rands. A mine that had security issues they didn't seem to be doing anything to rectify. The scary thing was those two had made themselves into billionaires' through the connections of their families, which in my book, is some form of corruption. They later promised they were going to donate some percentage to charities over the years to come. The truth is; it was just some way to ease up the pressure. Nothing will really filter through to the poor of South Africa. These newly rich blacks are not helping much in the development of the society. There are not many scholarships, academic trusts, endowments or grants in South African education, research etc..., from these newly rich blacks, as compared to what is obtaining across the colour divide.

A year down the line, Aurora mine has now been closed, making redundant 5 300 workers, who haven't been paid for nearly a year now. They can't even access their pensions which the directors of the company (Kulubuse Zuma, Zondwa Mandela, Max Hulley and others) mismanaged. The galling thing is that they are being protected from corruption charges because of their connection to the ruling class. The scale at which these politicians are amassing wealth rivals what I saw in Zimbabwe through these BEE deals.

Robert Guest notes in his book, "The Shackled Continent" that "a favoured place on the perimeter of the trough is not gender specific and the wives of those aptly described as "the new Jacobins" are not precluded from getting their snoots on the gravy." He also notes that the western world has accepted as the cost of doing business in South Africa is to bribe the politicians. Some bribes are as hefty as 9 billion dollars! Michela Wrong's analysis of the same era in Zaire (DRC) offers some wonderful insights into Africa's black empowerment policies. In her book, "In the footsteps of Mr Kurtz", Michela Wrong traces the origin of the term "grosses legumes", that is, "big vegetables."

This lexicon was devised by the poor Zairians witnessing the elite newly rich blacks amassing wealth on a sick proportion whilst they were getting poorer and poorer. Big vegetables, I would like to think of a big cabbage on some fertile spot of land, being fed enough water and other nutrients for some months, growing bigger and bigger, without giving anything back. It's the same description the Zairians had about their newly rich elite. Michela Wrong notes that "In 1973, Mobuto decreed that foreign owned firms, farms, plantations, etc, which were mostly owned by foreigners (Portuguese, Italian, Greeks, Pakistani and many other traders) should be returned over to the sons of the country. The result was an obscene scramble for freebies by the burgeoning Zairian elite…" The social class known as the "grosses legumes" was coined.

The ordinary Zairians watched stupefied as business closed, prices rocketed, jobs were doled out as reward on nepotistic lines and the shelves emptied. After wasting their newly found riches on luxuries (Zaire held the record for the highest purchases of the Mercedes luxury vehicles in Africa, at that time), the big vegetables could be

170

heard asking when the Portuguese or Greek owners were returning back to stock their warehouses. With nowhere else to buy the stock (the parent companies of these confiscated business had cut credit lines), or because of lack of cash investments through mismanagement of these companies, these big vegetables could only close shop, thereby impacting on the ordinary Zairians. I believe these big vegetables form the bulk of the Zairians in western capitals like Paris, yet the ordinary folks didn't have anywhere to go but to face the effects of this Zairenization of the economy.

The same thing has happened with Zimbabwe through its chaotic Land Reform Program, and now it has been expanded into mining and manufacturing industries expropriation, with catastrophic effects. Mozambique did its own form of this Zairenization in the 1970s, through the nationalisation of all the companies. Up until now, Mozambique hasn't been able to reverse the effects of this misguided endeavour, but it learned its lessons well. It is now one country, in the Southern Africa region, that is becoming a safe haven of whites leaving Zairenization happening in South Africa and Zimbabwe. Due to that, its economy is growing very rapidly.

Zairenization in Zaire fostered the belief on the entire country that some things could be had for nothing. The looter's smash-and-grab mentality had been endorsed at the highest level of the society. In South Africa, they are now doing the same thing, saintly, through their BEE. It is a softened, legally induced handover of the same proportion.

Another huge issue doing South Africa is skills shortages. Health professionals (doctors, nurses, technicians etc...) are leaving. It is estimated that they are over 31 000 nursing posts vacant. Over 5

KZN hospitals have been closed or are functioning minimally due to skills shortage. This skills shortages has resulted in shocking infant mortality, maternity mortality, and life expectancy rates have plummeted to as low as 47 years, due to also because of the HIV scourge (Over 6 million South Africans have died from AIDS, the economically active, and more than 5 million are the recorded infected.) The latest statistics show that the doctors are leaving in droves to countries like Canada where they are offered better working conditions. They are offered three times better salaries, plus a bonus double their pay every 1-2 years, not to mention better lifestyles there in Canada. Hospitals and clinics are collapsing. Municipalities are also collapsing due to the leaving for greener pasture of trained engineers, technicians and managers. In the Eastern Cape, all or most, of the municipalities are dysfunctional.

The skills shortage has largely been due to migration, to first world countries, of South Africa's skilled productive part of the population. I have dealt with some numbers of South Africans who have left their country in another piece, *First impressions- a letter from South Africa*. Over 1 million former South Africans stay in the UK alone, and more than a million now live in other countries like the USA, Canada, Australia, New Zealand etc... Those who leave are between 20-40 years old, with their children, thus the most economically productive, thus it shrinks the tax base of South Africa, as well as creating skills shortages. The ANC has been creating, like apartheid South Africa, a new Diaspora with similarly race based labour laws.

People have been leaving South Africa feeling pushed not only by the fear of crime but they are concerned about affirmative action, unstable job markets, soaring house prices, unstable currency and inflation, popular homophobia and xenophobia, dealt with in the

172

piece, *There is no xenophobia in South Africa*. People also leave for a host other reasons like the desire to see the world (South Africans were not allowed to visit other countries because of their apartheid laws and system, so now they are taking the opportunity to do that). Some people also leave due to extended family ties abroad, better support of managing a disability and also, they could not shake the fear of being raped or hijacked. 1 500 white farmers have been killed in their homes since 1994, not to mention those raped. Farmers in South Africa are also leaving, and over 20 000 farmers have left for Mozambique and other surrounding countries, bar Zimbabwe, who dished out 4 000 white farmers. These farmers also complain of, on top of the killings and rape, low import tariffs and the dumping of cheap agric imports from the countries where farmers there are heavily subsidized. But, all in all, the biggest culprit why people are leaving, especially the white population is as I have noted due to race-based and transformation laws.

The laws are such that skilled white South Africans are now second choice for consideration of employment, especially in the public sector domain, and the public sector is the biggest employer. First preference is given to black South Africans. These laws have nothing to do with how skilled would be the blacks. Most of these black employees are political appointees who are not really skilled for the jobs. I won't say that they are no blacks who are skilled, no. There are there, in actual fact a lot, but they are also over-looked for political appointees. These have ultimately left the country for greener pastures, as well. These political appointees can only run down to dysfunctional those companies they have been given to manage.

Transformation is not about service delivery. It is not about a responsive government that provides services promptly, efficiently

173

and respectfully to the public. Transformation in South Africa is not about a police force that is incorrupt, and good at preventing crime. Transformation in South Africa is not about a health service sector that serves the sick efficiently. It is about head count, i.e., how many blacks, and how black is the black appointed. It is about the ANC black, or any other black.

This is exacerbated by the fact that South Africa, even though it is the most developed country in sub Saharan Africa, lags behind a lot of African countries in training technical, mathematical, scientific, and engineering students. In the "2007 IMD world competitiveness yearbook" South Africa, even though it is the 26th biggest economy in the world, was among the 55 countries with the highest brain drains and worst skills shortage. This is hardly surprising. It is a result of a failed education system producing maths, science and technical skills deficient students who can't even compete with other African countries, despite its more advanced status. This is the result of an alienating affirmative action program and aggressive black empowerment that promotes unqualified blacks regardless of merit. Here is a scenario I would like to explore.

Zimbabwe, even though it is by far poor as compared to South Africa developmentally, even though it has its own political problems that have bedevilled it for many years now, but in terms of education and skills training, it is ahead of South Africa. Its literacy rate is better than that of South Africa. There are about 23 universities in South Africa compared to 13 in Zimbabwe, South Africa doesn't have many technical or poly technical colleges, yet Zimbabwe has at least 10. South Africa doesn't have teachers training colleges, yet Zimbabwe has at least 12, whilst South Africa doesn't have any nurses training institutions, Zimbabwe has many, in fact, every general hospital in

174

Zimbabwe trains nurses. To add to the above, there are many agricultural colleges in Zimbabwe, many vocational training colleges, and many private colleges that offer internationally recognised courses. There are also vast training schemes in industry, like apprenticeship training and graduate trainee programmes. Contrast the information I have given you above versus the populations, land coverage, and GDP of these countries. Zimbabwe has a quarter of South Africa's population and land mass. Zimbabwe doesn't even have 5per cent of South Africa's GDP economy. This could go a long way in explaining why South Africa has skills shortages.

Another of South Africa's political schizophrenic characteristic of Zimbabwe is its sick obsessiveness with the transformation of the judiciary. Transformation of the judiciary by the ANC has been all about extending its power tentacles over all levers of power than with empowerment of the breath of the South African citizenry. The government has been appointing judges sympathetic to its ideology, judges who would toe the line. The appointment of the current Chief Justice did not follow merit, proven experience and competence, local and international repute. Authority and respect of seniority are no longer absolutes requirements. This process of judicial succession that required wise and sensitive management divided the country and rendered redundant an important public institution of democracy and the Judicial Service Commission (JSC).

There was only one preferred choice. There were also phenomena of informal circles of support, or the lack of it, around the pressure of a declared presidential preference. Now the country and its new Chief Justice have to live with a deeply divided public opinion. The issue is not about the capabilities of Justice Mogoeng Mogoeng, but of how public systems were broken to the detriment of public opinion.

175

Zimbabwe did this mass mobilization and social engineering to its judiciary with disastrous consequences. In south Africa, there is a concerted move to have black judges constituting the majority judges in its justice system. White judges who are perceived to be unfavourable to the ANC policies haunted out. A case in point is judge Hillary Squires who was haunted out by Mbeki. Zuma is currently working on Moseneke whom he over looked for the appointment to the Chief Justice position.

The two have a sour relationship that goes back to during the years of the liberation fight against apartheid. They were from opposing football teams at Robin Island, and Moseneke was the head of the football association there, whilst Zuma was his junior. Later, when Moseneke was the deputy Chief Justice, Zuma made a complaint about an election result in his KwaZulu Natal province, where he thought there was rigging in favour of the IFP, who had won the province. Moseneke didn't follow the complaint through, thus defeating Zuma's aspirations to be the premier of KwaZulu Natal. Zuma still holds Moseneke responsible for trying to scuttle his political career and many other fractions in his trials.

What that means is that the judges and the judiciary have to now be obligated to the executive, not to uphold the country's constitutional democracy based on equality for all, the rule of law, and the independence of the judiciary and separation of powers is eroded. Both Zuma and Moseneke, even South Africa, have to learn fast that justice and fairness are distributed values. They follow a simple ethical rule; do unto others as you would have them do unto you. This law gives us the basis on which to build a shared public life; inspires confidence, and widen loyalty to public office beyond sectarian loyalties that exclude.

Zuma has not only been appointing his favoured judges to the constitutional and Supreme Court, but as well, the NPA (National Prosecuting Authority), Police etc... The Police boss is a political appointee, not a professional policeman. The government (ANC) should learn to live with the gory side of the negotiations deal that ushered majority rule, by accepting all the compromises forged at CODESA, and get on with their lives because this continuous stereotyping of whites silences their right to democratic citizenship, like what Mugabe did to Zimbabwean whites.

Prioritization of the Defence ministry over the real economic ministries is another problem. In 2004, the government prioritised 44 billion Rands in the Arms deal when they were many other developmental needs that got lip service. This arms budget, and the arms deal, was fraught with irregularities, loopholes, corruption and has bedevilled politicians ever since. South Africa has huge delivery issues like the burgeoning poverty which I have noted in the piece, *First impression- a letter from South Africa*. South Africa is the most unequal society on earth having surpassed Brazil to this proud mantle. And there is a good direct link between crime and inequality. The most likely to suffer from this crime resultant from inequality are black African immigrants.

Whilst we are still on inequality, I think the ANC government has to figure out how they are going to distribute the economic pie, as soon as possible. This is the biggest threat to South Africa now. Blacks are still downtrodden, and a lot are still staying in shack towns all over South Africa's urban areas. If there has to be land reform, or any wealth distribution program that needs to be done, it should be initiated now, and be done in a sane, constructive way. The alternative is for the ANC government to try to create a high economic growth rate, in their economy, so that it would filter through to the poor, and raise a lot people into the middle class, especially the blacks. Without of which, it spells doom for South Africa.

There is also rapid increase in HIV infections rate, escalating crimes, abuse of children and women (every 1 in 4 South African men are potential rapists. There is also a court case of Jub Jub (a singer) who killed 4 students and injured 2 in Soweto whilst doing street racing with his friend (Shabalala), in the afternoons, on a major South African road.), drug abuse, high unemployment rates, endless cash-in-transit heist, and countless other ills it has to solve very soon.

No cabinet minister was fired for being incompetent and useless in South Africa up until 2010 from 1994, even the much ridiculed Manto Shabalala Msimang (Health minister, in the Mbeki administration who refused to roll out anti-retroviral drugs saying she favoured traditional medicines, in which over 350 000 deaths occurred due to this late response.) was protected by Mbeki, and was kept in government by Zuma. Over half of the cabinet under Mbeki deserved to be fired. This lack of delivery from the ministers and government is invoking mass protests and anger. Public resentment is so palpable and this is confirmed by the increasing number of service delivery protests, or even at that, Union strikes. This is a very dangerous precursor to what the future holds for South Africa. The people are becoming more and more aware of their situation.

In order to deflect this pressure away from the government, there is this sick, "proudly South African campaign", coined to encourage nationalism that is vacuous and is a part of myth making

178

characteristic of the discourse of spin doctors. Jonathan Moyo, in Zimbabwe, devised many of these "proudly Zimbabwean campaigns", with endless songs and convoluted speeches, on being proudly Zimbabwean. It was such a sick thing to have to deal with, sometimes every five minutes, on the television and radio. South Africa, unlike Zimbabwe, should know that pride must be earned.

There are a lot other issues that link with what I have dealt with in this essay, but I believe these are some of the most important things South Africa has to deal with, to stop this doing of South Africa. To conclude this essay I will use the words of Njabulo. S. Ndebele. "The time has come for people in South Africa to reconnect with their truest aspirations to restore their constitutional compass, to restore authority, to restore dignity in public institutions, to restore merit as the criterion for achieving excellence in service, to create wealth honestly, to work hard and increase productivity for the common good, to heal the public lives and appreciate one another more, to restore peaceful protest, to teach and guide their children, and care for the sick under all circumstances, to recover shame and conscience, to restore their deepest sense of honour, purpose, and conviction, which have been the foundation of 100 years of organised service in pursuit of justice and human dignity. "The Sunday Times, October 2, 2011.

The job now lies in South Africans' hands. They have to regain their moral and ethical authority through scrutinizing their leaders, and choose the right leaders in the next elections.

Post-Power Sharing Deal Rhetoric

I n Zimbabwe we need a dream and hope. Obama and the new administration, please help.... Desperate, The Citizen, 21 January 2009.

Mugabe's illegitimate government invites the MDC, who are legitimate, to become accomplices in Mugabe dictatorship...No deal, The Citizen, 20 January 2009.

At last "The Citizen" got it right by naming Mugabe for what he is, a dictator, in the lead-in clip on page one of yesterday's edition. But then your journalist recants by calling him president in the two articles on page seven. Inconsistent to say the least....John Fenwick, The Citizen, 21 January 2009.

It boggles the mind that there are South Africans calling for our government to break relations with Israel, thousands of kilometres away, yet who are mum about atrocities conducted against ordinary folk in Zimbabwe by a cruel self-centred dictator who has absolutely no sympathy with, nor feelings for, his subjects. Talk of double standards....J S Pietersen, The Citizen, 20 January 2009.

Southern Africa deserves Mad Grace and her despot husband since it seems to support their antics, including raping the country....Dave, The Citizen, 20 January 2009.

Please Zuma go to court for your corruption. You can't be the president in South Africa; this is not Zimbabwe....M Magaga, The Citizen 21 January 2008.

We haven't done enough but we are among those who have decided we will no longer be silent. The numbers (who have died in Zimbabwe), are not very different from Darfur, they are not different from what happened in Rwanda. This is not normal.... Graca Machel, The Star, 22 January 2009.

Reconciliation is the key in Zimbabwe.... Carolina, The Citizen, 20 January 2009.

Zimbabwe has "reached a situation where an executive authority completely ignores the orders of the courts, thus placing itself above the law, able to do whatever it wishes to citizens, ignoring all laws and constitutional rights, abusing its powers at will and with impunity".... Zimbabwe Legal Resources Foundation, The Star, 22 January 2009

Unity Deal Uludes Zim Again As Mp's Balk "The proposed constitutional amendment Zimbabwe's parliament refused to take was needed to make a power sharing agreement a reality, by creating a prime minister's post in the Unity government. This is after Mugabe and opposition factions ended 12 hours of talks with no progress on the unity deal. A special regional summit was set next week to try to break the deadlock. The MDC accuses Mugabe of trying to retain too many key cabinet and government posts in any Unity government, and of undermining the spirit of the agreement signed in September by harassing, beating and killing opposition supporters and human rights activists"....The Star, 21 January 2009.

Those outstanding issues need to be addressed before we accept the amendment.... Alexander Masundire, MDC MP, The Star, 21 January 2009.

A southern African development community summit on Zimbabwe will probably take place in Joburg on Monday, after Robert Mugabe refused to have it in Botswana... The Star, 22 January 2009.

Salamao, SADC executive secretary, warned that the summit would be the SADC's last effort to break the deadlock.... The Citizen, 27 January 2009.

The way forward after this summit, whether there is an agreement or there is no agreement, President Mugabe is going to form a cabinet... Bright Matonga, Deputy Information Minister, The Citizen, 27 January 2009.

We are worlds apart... MDC official at the summit. The Citizen 27 January 2009.

This Maybe The Last Chance

After an all-night meeting, president Kgalema Motlanthe, current chairman of the Southern African Development Community(SADC), announced early on Tuesday that the SADC heads of states and the three Zimbabwean political leaders had agreed that the long-delayed power sharing Unity government in that country would be launched early next month.... But then members of Morgan Tsvangirai's MDC immediately disputed that interpretation of the marathon meeting in Pretoria, saying the MDC had agreed to no such thing and that the SADC leaders had fallen far short of the MDC demands. And official statement from MDC spokesperson Nelson Chamisa, though reiterating that the summit had fallen "far short of our expectations" did not reject the SADC communiqué explicitly. He said that the MDC's National Council would meet on Friday "to define the party's position".... The Star, 29 January 2009.

It seems Tsvangirai agreed to go into the unity government, not because he likes the deal, but because he suspects that is the best he will get and that something has to be done to stop the rot in his country. But hardliners like MDC secretary general Tendai Biti undercut him.... It would be short sight for all the MDC leadership not to realise that is the farthest the negotiations have gone, and that this maybe the time to reach a final agreement to pull their country back from the precipice... The Star, 29 January 2009.

Zimbabwe president Robert Mugabe has sworn in his long-time rival Morgan Tsvangirai as prime minister, ushering in a Unity government in an extra-ordinary concession after nearly three decades of virtually unchallenged rule... The Star, 12 February 2009.

Tsvangirai said he knew many were, "sceptical of this agreement. But this is the only viable arrangement we have"... Tsvangirai, The Star, 12 February 2009.

It depends on how co-operative Mugabe is and whether he can be trusted. Mugabe no longer has absolute power, and that could be the turning point... Ian Stephens, Harare Businessman, The Star, 12 February 2009.

I am happy because I expect the prices to go down. They have got to get the schools and hospitals working again… Simpson Ibrahim, Street vendor, Harare, The Star, 12 February 2009.

Their swearing in was "an important milestone towards the formation of an inclusive government as the people of Zimbabwe march towards national reconciliation, economic recovery, reconstruction and development"… President Kgalema Motlanthe, The Star, 12 February 2009.

Yesterday's announcement of the appointment of permanent secretaries is in contravention of the global political agreement and the constitution of Zimbabwe, which is very clear with regard to senior government appointments… Tsvangirai, The Star, 26 February 2009.

Mugabe has illegally appointed 10 more ZANUPF cabinet ministers. Farm invasions have re-started. The Zimbabwe "Unity" government is now controlled by Mugabe and his cronies. Nothing has changed except that MDC has been destroyed all with the help of the SADC and ANC… P Joffe, The Citizen, 26 February 2009.

"I don't care whether the cat is brown or black, as long as it catches mice. We don't care where (the aid) comes from". Tsvangirai after being asked whether he would consider British aid… The Star, 23 February 2009.

The UN chief said support for Zimbabwe would be forthcoming if progress was made in implementing the September 2008 power sharing agreement. "All these efforts would be better mobilised and

184

would get stronger (and more) support from the international community if we can see the progress in political and national reconciliation. Releasing political leaders would be important and desirable. That said, I remain concerned about the arrest and detention of human rights defenders. I hope these people will be freed as soon as possible"... Ban Ki-moon UN Secretary General. The Citizen, 26 February 2009.

Mugabe Is Still The Problem

"The man who stole the election is still calling the shots at the negotiating table, and is allowed to engage in acts of brinkmanship as he did this week when he threatened to pull out of talks and announce his own cabinet that would exclude the MDC. But the most importantly, Mugabe has three MPs from the MDC- Broadwin Nyaude, Matthias Mlambo and Pearson Mungofa- arrested on Tuesday, bringing to five the total number of arrested MDC MPs." The Sunday Times Editor's Comment (31 August 2008)

I am writing this essay piece in November 2011, after almost three years of the power sharing arrangement in Zimbabwe. Mugabe is still the problem! Not only that; Mugabe is the problem, as well as the solution. Mugabe is running the country and cabinet all alone, with the exception of, maybe, the finance ministry. Tendai Biti, the Finance Minister, seems to have a good grip on his ministry, and thus he always angers the ZANUPF establishment and Mugabe. Biti is the only minister who is mostly demonized by the public media from the MDC. Even his boss, Morgan Tsvangirai, the president of the MDC, is less demonized these days than Biti. Tsvangirai is simply overshadowed by Mugabe, so he should be feeling like a junior partner in this dispensation, or even at that, an un-trusted deputy to Mugabe.

Mugabe is old and unstable, which is a very dangerous thing to the country. Even the former Army General who was murdered politically, a couple of months ago, by being burned in an inferno of fire to beyond recognition, in his farm house in the Beatrice farming area, obviously in power or political killings games of the ZANUPF, Mujuru, feels that Mugabe is too old and unstable. Former Army General Mujuru, he was the husband of the vice president, Joyce Mujuru, and has been known as the head of the Mujuru faction, which is fighting for power against the Mnangagwa faction, said that in the Wiki-leaks cables, being published on the internet. He said that it is increasingly becoming obvious that only Mugabe's drive, not the entire ZANUPF party (who seem to want the old leader out, as well), is directing and controlling the destiny of the country, and the party. He has help from the top Army Generals, Police top brass and the CIO. Mujuru said Mugabe is too old and unstable, to be leading the country; and some even say he is insane.

There is no doubt that Mugabe is a very complex character. One moment, he can behave like an astute fatherly figure, and the next moment, he is like those crazy cruel little boys, and then like an incarnation of Hitler, then like a jocular harmless old man. It just depends with the mood he would be in, and what he would get by behaving whichever way he would be behaving. In doing all that, he has been running the country episodically, according to his moods, by pushing policies that are insane and destabilizing to the country, like the indigenization law, negotiations on the elections and power sharing issues, for instance. Even his illness affects him episodically (periodic convulsions, stroke like episodes (perhaps ischemia brought on by diabetes or lipid disorder that effects the cover of the brain; this is according to his doctors, in the Wiki-leaks cables). Some even speculate the old man is being chewed by prostate cancer, without qualification, though. And so, he has been running the country half asleep, half awake.

Even the president of Botswana, Ian Khama, said that at one of their SADC meetings on Zimbabwe that Mugabe was dozing most of the times and, would wake up once in a while to answer questions. Not that I blame him for doing that. I believe there is not much that SADC is worth staying awake for, at their meetings. Mugabe knows that there is nothing this ineffective group could do to him, that's why after nearly 10 years; this body hasn't been able to totally solve the Zimbabwean issue, neither to push Mugabe to implement the agreements of the GNU. So that, for over ten years now, prior to the year 2000 madness, Mugabe has been running the country like that, episodically; without much listening to advice from anyone else because he will be asleep most of the times. This has been the pace at which the country has been functioning, half asleep, half awake, episodically.

He would select one ZANUPF leader he would put in a powerful ministry, and in the front, and who would do the dirty work for him. This leader would become the de-facto, powerful (prime) minister. Mugabe would allow this leader a lot of leverage, to work across ministries and broader functions, not just their ministries or departments. Jonathan Moyo, Joyce Mujuru, Gideon Gono (Reserve Bank governor), and lately Mnangagwa (Defence minister) are some of the examples. These leaders would cover for Mugabe whilst he sleeps and, they are mostly chosen because they have done one or another misdemeanour that could have had them arrested. But mostly because they are incompetent and unprofessional, so in exchange of their ineptitude and prosecution, they would be made to pay through this narcissistic exploitation. Until their usage-by-date

188

has come up, in which they will be excreted as waste, maybe until another resuscitation time. Jonathan Moyo has been making ingratiating moves towards this resuscitating; by being such a sick sycophant for Mugabe, supporting Mugabe to the hilt, in his pathetic speeches on the television.

This power structure system being used by Mugabe has created such a complex governance issue and system in Zimbabwe, both in the government and the party. ZANUPF is now some huge monster without a central place (brain), but with a lot of conflicting, confusing and corrosive parts, that are difficult to exploit and work with from the outside, even from the inside. That's why the power sharing negotiations or Mugabe's successor debates haven't been able to accrue a lot of progress. That (the successor debate), in itself, is a politically explosive time bomb, if it's not dealt with foresight. The country needs Mugabe to be alive for the elections and post elections period, or for him to pick up an acceptable, to both camps, successor before the elections to avoid plunging the party into a killing orgy, and the country into anarchy. Going by the Wiki-leaks cables, the doctors of Mugabe are saying he won't be alive past 2013, which is another headache, and another Mugabe problem. The cold reality is we need free and fair elections as soon as possible. It's an incredible reality considering the things that have to happen before any election could be held.

The second biggest Mugabe problem is the partisan way in which the defence, security and police apparatus in Zimbabwe is still supporting the ZANUPF (Mugabe), not securing the country as their mandate dictates. The service chiefs still brazenly support ZANUPF, and have refused to recognize the MDC as a legitimate opposition or partner. Some have gone to the extent of saying they would never salute

Tsvangirai, if he wins elections and automatically becomes the commander-in-chief of the defence forces, head of state and the government. They still view Tsvangirai as a western puppet, not a genuine opposition leader, mandated by the Zimbabwean electorate. As long as this is the status quo, there is no election that ZANUPF will lose, that they will accept. This is why the MDC has been pushing for security sector reforms.

It seems Mugabe is still a hostage president, with Mnangagwa as a de-facto prime minister. You can get the sense of this because at every SADC meeting or mediation effort, the defence minister is attending these days, as if he is trying to make sure the military junta's position is respected and instituted in the negotiations. The security apparatus and Mugabe are thwarting these security sector reforms, the constitution creation, and the GNU government's work. It is increasingly becoming obvious that it will be difficult for the GNU government to comply with all the agreements of the global political agreement (GPA), that ushered this GNU government, without which, it would be very difficult to carry out a free and fair election in Zimbabwe. Mugabe has repeatedly refused any security, media, and ZEC (Zimbabwe Electoral Commission) reforms, even though they are part of the GPA agreements, among others.

Another equally huge issue related to the above issue is the psyche of the Zimbabweans. There are those who don't give a damn anymore about the country, those who don't care who wins, Mugabe or Tsvangirai? Most of whom, were supporters of the opposition parties. They are not going to vote. In their psyche there are tired of getting a raw deal (cheating) from these electoral endeavours. Then there are those who are scared of political violence. In their psyche there is going to be violence. This group touches a huge chunk of the electorate. They won't vote, or maybe they will vote, but still thinking that they will be violence after or even before the elections. It is in their minds. Psychologically, both groups are not ready for elections by any stretch. There is an urgent need for the reconciliation and healing process to happen, maybe for a tribunal along the South African's lines, to be instituted and to work to heal these destroyed and flawed victims.

The ministry and government department responsible for this hasn't done much, so also, the GPA leaders. They have to dedicate most of their electioning time towards campaigns for a free and fair elections, for violence free environment, for reconciliation, for national healing. The biggest problem is it hasn't happened between Mugabe and Tsvangirai. That's where it should begin. They have to forgive each other genuinely, reconcile, embrace each other genuinely and work together as a people mandated by the electorate. If it doesn't happen between them, it won't happen downstream, thus the election is going to be unfair, violent and destructive, and the country won't re-normalize.

Another key Mugabe problem is his refusal to implement media reforms by opening the media to private players, especially the electronic media which is 100per cent owned and controlled by ZANUPF, through, of course, the public broadcaster, ZBC. These public Medias constitute about 80per cent coverage of Zimbabwe. The ZANUPF and Mugabe should also allow the journalist at the public Medias to do their jobs professionally, without toeing to the party's line. The media is still shut out to the opposition. They can only be opened to the MDC when they are criticizing or demonizing it. It is still all about securing Mugabe. If you listen and watch, or read the public media output, you would be mistaken to think that

Mugabe is just coming into power, as if it's not the same Mugabe who destroyed the country for the past 31 years. Even deputy ministers from the ZANUPF, in ministries that the MDC controls are featured better than their bosses, in these public Medias. This full throttle control Mugabe has on the public media will make campaigning or access of the electorate untenable for the other parties in the electioning period next year, or beyond that.

Another equally related problem is that of ZEC, and the electoral laws. They have to be reformed, well before any credible election. This body (ZEC) has to be made up of non-political figures who are appointed by the parliament, not the presidency. This body, the voters roll and the electoral laws are lopsided on the side of the ZANUPF party. In an April 2010 audit of the voters roll carried out by the Zimbabwe Election Support Network (ZESN), the country's election watchdog; it showed that at least 27 per cent of voters registered in the current voters roll are deceased and only 18per cent of those registered are youths aged between18-30. So ZEC has to do a meticulous editing and sorting of this voter's roll before any elections.

The biggest headache for everyone in Zimbabwe should be the constitution making process that has bedevilled the nation for the past two years. It has been fraught with disturbances, illegality, and corruption. Adding to the suppression of people's views at the outreach stage, the collation stage of the process has been viewed as an indirect attempt by political parties to influence the content, further reducing the credibility of the whole process. The draft that would come out, eventually, might not really represent Zimbabweans' aspirations. There wasn't even a representative outreach programme, and most of the views were disregarded in the making of this constitution. There have also been arguments on whether they should use more of qualitative, or more of quantitative methods of data interpretation, with the ZANUPF favouring quantitative, and the MDC favouring more of qualitative methods.

The other constitutional headache is; it is being crafted by politicians who would try to entrench their political ideologies and needs in the constitution, not those that are altruistic for the country, and future focused. This constitution should be about the future, not the past. We are not living in the past. It is the future we should be anticipating. According to the views on the late, former Justice of South Africa, Ismael Mohammed, a country's constitution, "is not simply a structure which mechanically defines the structures of government and the relation between the government and the governed, it is a "mirror of the national soul", the identification of the ideals and aspirations of a nation, the articulation of the values binding its people and disciplining its government." So it seems, this mirror of our national soul is going to be the demon we would have to live with.

Another key area that works hand in hand with the constitution making is the concern on the uncertainty of the elections and election date. Mugabe was adamant for most of the year that it should be held this year, but now he has set his sights for March 2012. He said, constitution or no constitution, elections are going to be held next March. To begin with, it's even difficult to be sure there will be a constitution by then. It also brings to light that Mugabe wants to put all the other issues of the GPA into insignificance, as if the GPA had been about the constitution only. There is still the issue of the media

193

reforms, security sector reforms, ZEC reforms to be addressed to make the environment conducive for an election that is free and fair. Dealing with all these issues requires more time and compromise, and it's likely the election will happen somewhere end 2012 or in 2013, which Mugabe doesn't want to hear of.

His other problematic finger is now immersed in the indigenization issue. Land barons like the co-home affairs minister are still willy-nilly appropriating land without respect of their own Land Reform Act; taking land from small scale black farmers which had been given to these farmers legally, in the Beitbridge area. The senator president has upped the ante in the mining sector by appropriating mines and mining claims from fellow blacks, hiding behind the indigenization law and requirements. Big business, the main owners of the industries and mines, the core of the country's economic recovery, are now sceptical about investing in Zimbabwe with the environment obtaining because of this indigenization law. In the budget calendar year 2011-2012, Zimbabwe could only attract about 300 million dollars in foreign direct investment, when a smaller country like Mozambique attracted over 2 billion dollars of foreign direct investment. These foreign (direct investors) and firms have been threatened with closure of their companies, through the revoking of their trading licences by the "irrationally exuberant" indigenization minister (Savious Kasukuwere) if they fail to fulfil the 51per cent local ownership.

This law has also divided the unity government, with the MDC against it because it would reverse economic gains that have been made so far. Like the land reform of year 2000, which was used to cow the white commercial farmers into submission, or to push them out of the country because of their alignment and support of the MDC, this indigenisation and expropriation of big business is being done with the same spirit. The big businesses have never supported ZANUPF so that expropriation is being done to weaken them and twist them so that in the next elections, through cash bequest, as a thank-you to Mugabe and the ZANUPF, they would finance the ZANUPF.

Another Mugabe problem is that of the blood diamonds trade of the Marange killing fields. A lot of money from diamond is not being channelled into the official channel, the treasury. The illegal trade has defrauded the country of over 2 billion dollars-worth of this precious revenue earner, a lot of which is lining up the pockets of ZANUPF bigwigs and party. The money will definitely be used for campaigns next year, for human rights abuses; not to even mention that there are still grave human rights abuses in the Marange fields. The killing of Tsorosai Kusena (Sept 2011) by the police, and his brothers are still recovering from injuries inflicted by the police, is a good example.

As long as draconian laws like POSA (Public Order Security Act) which is used to deny opposition parties the right to assemble, by the police, without a good enough reason from the police, and AIPPA (Access to Information Protection and Privacy Act), used to silence media people from publishing and broadcasting articles that are critical of the government, Mugabe and the ZANUPF are still there, there won't be any fair elections. All these have been used, and are still being used, to silence and harass the MDC officials, even those in the GNU entity by the partisan police, army and security apparatus. As we move towards elections there is resurfacing of political violence along party-lines, arbitrary arrests, detention, torture and

195

extra-judicial killings. The question on everyone lips is "what wrong did Jestina Mukoko do, and who killed Mujuru?

No one knows, let alone the families of these people.

Mmap Nonfiction and Academic books

If you have enjoyed *Zimbabwe: The Blame Game*, consider these other fine *Nonfiction and Academic* books from Mwanaka Media and Publishing:

Cultural Hybridity and Fixity by Andrew Nyongesa
Tintinnabulation of Literary Theory by Andrew Nyongesa
South Africa and United Nations Peacekeeping Offensive Operations by Antonio Garcia
A Case of Love and Hate by Chenjerai Mhondera
A Cat and Mouse Affair by Bruno Shora
The Scholarship Girl by Abigail George
The Gods Sleep Through It All by Wonder Guchu
PHENOMENOLOGY OF DECOLONIZING THE UNIVERSITY: Essays in the Contemporary Thoughts of Afrikology by Zvikomborero Kapuya
Africanization and Americanization Anthology Volume 1, Searching for Interracial, Interstitial, Intersectional and Interstates Meeting Spaces, Africa Vs North America by Tendai R Mwanaka
Africa, UK and Ireland: Writing Politics and Knowledge Production Vol 1 by Tendai R Mwanaka
Writing Language, Culture and Development, Africa Vs Asia Vol 1 by Tendai R Mwanaka, Wanjohi wa Makokha and Upal Deb
Zimbolicious: An Anthology of Zimbabwean Literature and Arts, Vol 3 by Tendai Mwanaka
Drawing Without Licence by Tendai R Mwanaka
Writing Grandmothers/ Escribiendo sobre nuestras raíces: Africa Vs Latin America Vol 2 by Tendai R Mwanaka and Felix Rodriguez
Nationalism: (Mis)Understanding Donald Trump's Capitalism, Racism, Global Politics, International Trade and Media Wars, Africa Vs North America Vol 2 by Tendai R Mwanaka
It Is Not About Me: Diaries 2010-2011 by Tendai Rinos Mwanaka
Chitungwiza Mushamukuru: An Anthology from Zimbabwe's Biggest Ghetto Town by Tendai Rinos Mwanaka

The Day and the Dweller: A Study of the Emerald Tablets by Jonathan Thompson
Zimbolicious Anthology Vol 4: An Anthology of Zimbabwean Literature and Arts by Tendai Rinos Mwanaka and Jabulani Mzinyathi
Parks and Recreation by Abigail George
FAMILY LAW AND POLITICS WITH BIOLOGY AND ROYALTY IN AFRICA AND NORTH AMERICA by Peter Ateh-Afec Fossungo
Writing Robotics, Africa Vs Asia, Vol 2 by Tendai Rinos Mwanaka
Zimbolicious Anthology Vol 5: An Anthology of Zimbabwean Literature and Arts by Tendai R. Mwanaka
Love Notes: Everything is Love, An Anthology of Indigenous Languages of Africa and East Europe by Tendai R Mwanaka
Zimbolicious Anthology Vol 6: An Anthology of Zimbabwean Literature and Arts by Tendai R. Mwanaka and Chenjerai Mhondera
BATTLING LANGUAGE RIGHTS GOVERNANCE IN AFRICA: SWISSELGIANISM, UBACKISM, AND THE AMBAZONIA-CAMEROUN WAR by Peter Ateh-Afec Fossungo
Otherness and Pathology: The Fragmented Self and Madness in Contemporary African Fiction by Andrew Nyongesa

Upcoming
Zimbabwe: Beyond Robert Mugabe by Tendai Rinos Mwanaka
The Trick is to Keep Breathing: Covid 19 Stories From African and North American Writers, Vol 3 by Tendai Rinos Mwanaka
Recentring Mother Earth by Andrew Nyongesa
Zimbabwe: The Urgency Of Now, New and Recollected Essays and Non Fictions by Tendai Rinos Mwanaka
Language, Thought, Art and Existence: New and Recollected Essays and Non Fictions By Tendai Rinos Mwanaka
Experimental Writing, Africa Vs Latin America Vol 1 by Tendai Rinos Mwanaka and Ricardo Felix Rodriguez
Fixing Earth Anthology: An anthology of Africa, UK and Ireland Writers, Vol 2 by Tendai Rinos Mwanaka

https://facebook.com/MwanakaMediaAndPublishing/

Printed in the United States
by Baker & Taylor Publisher Services